A Life in Storytelling

A Life in Storytelling

Anecdotes, Stories to Tell, Stories with Movement and Dance, Suggestions for Educators

Binnie Tate Wilkin

ROWMAN & LITTLEFIELD
Lanham • Boulder • New York • Toronto • Plymouth, UK

Published by Rowman & Littlefield
4501 Forbes Boulevard, Suite 200, Lanham, Maryland 20706
www.rowman.com

10 Thornbury Road, Plymouth PL6 7PP, United Kingdom

British Library Cataloguing in Publication Information Available

Library of Congress Cataloging-in-Publication Data

Wilkin, Binnie Tate, 1933-
A life in storytelling : anecdotes, stories to tell, stories with movement and dance, suggestions for educators / Binnie Tate Wilkin.
pages cm
Includes bibliographical references and index.
ISBN 978-1-4422-3177-1 (pbk. : alk. paper) -- ISBN 978-1-4422-3178-8 (ebook) 1. Storytelling. 2. Folklore--Performance. 3. Movement (Acting) 4. Dance. I. Title.
1. Aesthetics. 2. Postmodernism. I. Rundell, John F. II. Title.
LB1042.W547 2014
372.67'7044--dc23
2013040157

Printed in the United States of America

To family, friends, students, and audiences who have listened to my stories for more than fifty years, responding with enthusiasm and nurturing the storyteller's desire to share. To teachers, librarians, and other adult leaders who provided opportunities for adventures in wonder and imaginary travel. To eager children, some now adults, who instinctively suspend disbelief knowing that the story is all people.

Contents

Foreword

Storytelling is essential to the human soul. We crave, live, and love stories. Sharing stories is the foundation of knowledge, information, awareness, and understanding. The telling of stories is for everyone of every hue and every part of the world, whether old, young, rich, or poor. We need to tell and hear stories aloud. Stories are our humanity. However, it is the storyteller who makes the magic happen.

Binnie Tate Wilkin is a master storyteller. Over the years, she has told stories throughout the continent. I have seen her mesmerize her audiences with her signature style of "stories with movement and dance," in which she fully involves her audiences, who leave with the euphoric feeling of having a richer and better human experience.

In her book *A Life in Storytelling*, professional storyteller Binnie Tate Wilkin shares with readers her valuable wisdom, knowledge, and experiences. She conveys how to choose and tell stories and how to develop a personalized storytelling style and provides practical recommendations for educators, parents, and adult leaders. This exciting volume features quality stories and tales as well as valuable resources and references.

This is an important book on the art and practice of storytelling and has an important place in our twenty-first-century lives. I am pleased and delighted that this essential work will be shared for present and future generations to enjoy.

Dr. Claudette Shackelford McLinn
Executive Director
Center for the Study of Multicultural Children's Literature
Inglewood, California

Introduction

Hot summer days and nights in the small North Carolina town where I was reared were spent on covered front porches. To avoid the dense, uncomfortable humidity inside, families gathered in wooden swings anchored on the ceiling and relaxed on comfortable porch chairs and lounges. If all seats were filled, children sat on stoops or porch edges. When joined by neighbors or other passersby, idle conversation and delicious hilarity sometimes ensued. Stories of that day's work, a happening in the family, or tales of hunting were told. Classic animal tales reminiscent of Aesop's fables and Br'er Rabbit motifs were common, as were *real* ghostly encounters with the spirit world. Tall tales of people who had *visions* and those with exceptional strength were very familiar. Outside play meant constant encounters with june bugs, bees, mosquitoes, and flies. At night, frogs were easily found hopping underneath the street lights. Fireflies flickered incessantly while the songs of birds and crickets provided background music for happy and sad stories told by adults. In particular, when aunts came to visit, family story competitions developed and involved slaps of hands, demonstrative shouts, and momentary struts. Hands on the hips accompanied stories, proverbs, and poetic wisdom. In such an atmosphere, with folklore a part of daily life, the probability was that an imaginative child always inventing and dreaming stories, like myself, would evolve into a storyteller. Once, after sitting on the stoop and spending many minutes stomping on huge black ants crawling from a large chinaberry tree, my dreams were of giant ants with large boots, invading the town and stamping out people! Repeating that dream to anyone who would listen to me began my training as a storyteller.

Originally I intended to become a teacher, but my first professional job was as an elementary school librarian. Reading aloud and telling stories to classes became routine. Later, specialization in children's services at the School of Library Science, State University of New York at Albany, provided formal information about using storytelling in classrooms and libraries. Before entering and during the master's program, my assignment as children's librarian in a small branch of the Schenectady County Public Library was a practical laboratory. Mornings, before opening to the community, this public library branch, which was located in a school, operated much like a school library. Classes from the school visited for routine library activities, including storytelling. From this time forward, storytelling became part of my life and career. At the Los Angeles City Public Library, when assigned to a federally funded library project as children's services specialist, my adventures with *story* and *dance* began. Courses taught at schools of library and information science included storytelling. Full- or part-time teaching assignments were served at the University of California at Los Angeles and at Berkeley; the University of Wisconsin, Milwaukee; Fullerton College; and Columbia University. Later, it was fascinating to assist in planning, tell stories, and perform in many ethnic communities, while immersed in multicultural programming at the Los Angeles County Public Library as the first and only minority services coordinator.

Some time ago, I told a story on *Chucko the Clown* and later on a local television program in Los Angeles. Numerous requests from head starts, schools, libraries, professional organizations, and the general public for workshops on storytelling were fulfilled over the years, the most recent of which was a series of workshops for the Salinas Public Library in 2007. Several workshops have been presented for the Unitarian Universalist Church of Las Vegas.

On two occasions, an invitation to perform for African American History Month was received from the Black History Department of East Carolina University in Greenville, North Carolina, my hometown. On one of those assignments, I was scheduled for several venues—a junior college, a high school, a radio interview, and storytelling at the high school, which was spotlighted on local television. After sessions, the front porch on which I relaxed was the same one of my childhood. Much had changed—most people had air conditioners and did not sit on porches as much as I remembered. People I knew and loved were no longer in the neighborhood to stop by for story sharing. Family and friends, known for years, appreciated my presence not so much as a performing storyteller but for stories remembered of times past.

This book, designed to share with persons exploring the art of storytelling, includes information and anecdotes from my experiences as teller and teacher. Having received many public requests for storytelling advice, I designed the book to be both inspirational and practical. Setting the stage with brief historical and cultural background information was presumed a necessity. Gleaned from notes retained from teaching, from expert storytellers, from folklorists, and from other sources, part I provides general, background information. Under the chapter titles "History, Life, and Culture," "Folklore Defined," and "Educational Value" are interpretive and intellectual expositions on storytelling. Oral discourse as a primary element in human development is explored. Part II begins with practical analyses and instructions for active tellers. "The Modern Storyteller" discusses the perennial question "What or who is a storyteller?" Advice is given about the complex task of "Choosing Stories to Tell," followed by "Reading, Adaptation, and Learning," illuminating the arduous task of accumulating a storyteller's repertoire. A chapter titled "Developing Personal Style" warning against imitation of others continues this section. My own style of presenting "Stories with Dance and Movement" is explained and detailed. Although professional storytellers do not focus on education, parents, librarians, teachers, and other interveners in children's lives often teach with stories. Part III, "Practical Uses and Resources," provides selected "Suggestions for Educators, Parents, and Adult Leaders," pointing them toward materials available on varieties of topics. "Stories to Tell" includes synopses or notes from my story files and other sources. Some classic titles are included for beginners, and "Three Original Stories" are added. Intended to be useful but not exhaustive is the selected list of "Resources, Organizations, References," including notes about storytelling festivals and interesting, helpful websites. The notes with these selections were prepared as an *extension of the text*, providing additional information in categories discussed elsewhere.

Preschool audiences are special. Their attention span is acutely short, and planning for storytelling with them is not covered in this volume. Some of the resources listed contain helpful information for working with this age group. "Personal Notes" are inserted throughout the book. These incidents and activities were chosen to instruct, to entertain, to present challenges, and to imprint in the mind of readers fragrant essences of the storytelling experience. The art of storytelling is considered that personal art that invites an audience to join the dance of life. Come, join the dance!

I

Storytelling: An Evolving Art

ONE

History, Life, and Culture

Before the arrival of the missionaries, if we asked, "By what were the stones made?" it was said, "They were made by Umvelinqangi." It is said that we men came out of a bed of reeds. When we asked, "By what was the sun made?" they said: "By Umvelinqangi." For we used to ask when we were little, thinking that the old men knew all things which are on the earth: yet forsooth they do not know; but we do not contradict them, for neither do we know. — Amazulu[1]

Storytellers all over the world were made guardians of history and moral law in the advent of scribes and printing. Memory was the main source for learning, with stories explaining everything, including all observable phenomena of nature. Storms, droughts, floods, volcanic eruptions, and other overwhelming events were relegated to numerous gods. Perhaps stories preserved families, calmed anxieties, and made heroic figures permanent idols. Pictographs, hieroglyphs, cave drawings, and relics tracing as far back as 15,000 BC document life in ancient times. Although much is unknown about ancient storytelling, evidence of narrations is reported to have been found in Mesopotamia from about 3000 BC.

At the British Science Festival of 2009, Dr. Jamshid (Jamie) Tehrani, a cultural anthropologist at Durham University, presented a paper finding variants of *Little Red Riding Hood* existing 2,600 years ago. His study included thirty-five variants of the well-known tale: "The oldest tale we found was an Aesopic fable that dated from about the sixth century BC, so the last common ancestor of all these tales certainly predated this. We are looking at a very ancient tale that evolved over time, Tehrani stated."[2] Closely related stories were found in Africa and in sister locations comprised of this group: Japan, Korea, China, and Burma. Samples resembling modern European versions were found in Nigeria and Iran. In a press interview, Tehrani was asked about the key finding of the work/research described in his presentation. His answer was:

> Folktales, like genes, are inherited from generation to generation. Some details are forgotten while others are added as they get told from person to person (the "Chinese Whispers Effect"). The gradual accumulation of modifications makes it possible to trace related stories back to their common source and identify "imaginative convergencies" in unrelated tales.[3]

For many years, historians indicated that the oldest surviving tale is Gilgamesh, twelve clay tablets relating the deeds of the famous Sumerian king of Uruk from approximately 2500 BC. In the epic of Gilgamesh, he is said to be one third man and two thirds god. Of interest in the story of Gilgamesh, a creation story appears similar to that of the Old Testament, book of Genesis. There are many fascinating likenesses in mythological stories from Greece and elsewhere that seem to replicate Bible stories. In one Greek myth, Zeus opens up the sky and allows the rain to fall and flood the land. Deucalion and Pyrrha escape in an ark that comes to rest at the top of a mountain.

EGYPT

Early records of storytelling were also found in Egypt. The annual flooding of the Nile was depicted and attributed to the minor Egyptian god Hapi. Egyptian papyri dating back to 2000 BC portray the sons of Cheops (the famous pyramid builder) taking turns entertaining their father with stories.

CHINA

Documents tracing oral history in Asia find storytelling was one of the many arts of the Zhou dynasty (1122–256 BC) and existing during the Han dynasty (206 BC–220 AD). In several sources, interesting descriptions of Chinese storytellers who performed in marketplaces or bazaars are recorded. *Pingtan* performers are said to have "depended on their mouths to eat," meaning they were paid for their storytelling. Among prevailing arguments is the declaration that early Chinese storytelling was more performance than *telling* because stories were memorized and recited with drama and music. Characteristic recitation of Buddhist epics included *pinghua* (storytelling or narration without music) and *tanci* (narration with music). Stories were often told in extended passages, with momentary breaks for music, humor, and poetry. During ancient times, a story could take as long as a month or more to tell.

JAPAN

Patterns similar to the Chinese style of storytelling seem apparent in Japanese storytelling. Ancient traditions relate to Buddhist and other religious practices, and in many stories, morals and events seemingly aimed at cultural cohesiveness are revealed. *Kamishibai*, the "poor man's theater," is said to have been created for ordinary citizens, imitating the picture-book storytelling tradition of illustrated scrolls related to Buddhist practices from as early as the ninth century. This style, sometimes called the first picture-book storytelling, flourished during the 1930s and during World War II. The 1920s to 1950s were the golden years of traveling storytellers who rode on bicycles, equipped with a box of drawers filled with candy and small hand-made stages built on top for showing cards with story text. Audiences were left with cliffhangers for the following week. This form disappeared after television became popular, but some revival has been seen in the twenty-first century.

Many stories for adults and children are linked to Hinamatsuri (Girls' Day) and other holiday celebrations. The story of "Momotaro" ("Little Peach Boy") has become a classic around the world, often compared to the European story of "Thumbelina." The Pandora-like theme of "opening the box" appears in the Japanese classic "Urashima Taro," about a fisherman who goes to sea and many years later returns to his village as youthful as when he left but finds no one he recognizes. Ignoring instructions *not* to open the box given to him by the prince, Urashima lifts the top and suddenly grows old with a long white beard. Inside, he has found his old age.

AFRICA

African traditions show reverence for stories and storytellers. In contradiction to popular misconceptions, ancient storytelling rituals existed on the African continent. While Africans are mostly oral peoples, complex cultures produced art forms that later became literary. Communal performance of stories and music, although varied, are important in most places. In urbanized locations today, rich oral arts of the past are regularly used on radio and television. Such countries as Kenya have taken steps to preserve and maintain cultural lore, and traditional stories may be found in school and university syllabi. Anne Pellowski, noted storyteller, lamented the fact that many cultural collections of stories in the United States have been thoroughly westernized. About Yoruba lore, she writes, "These tales may be told for the sheer enjoyment of the stories, or as one African way of explaining the actions of men and beasts, or to teach a moral in the Yoruba manner. When one can tell them with the perfect fusion of all of these purposes, one is close to being a Yoruba storytell-er."[4]

THE CARIBBEAN

Caribbean people have origins in many places, but their stories strongly reflect African cultural influences. Anansi (or Annancy in parts of the Caribbean) stories are popular there, but as is true around the world, fusion of cultures produced regional tricksters peculiar only to local peo-ple. In some locales, Anansi is replaced or joined by a human, adolescent, hero, and trickster called Ti Jean. Many specific demons, monsters, zom-bies, and spirits are recognizable by much of the populace. One is the Douennes (dwens), souls of children who have died before being bap-tized. Their souls wander in the wilderness and near rivers, with their feet turned backward and faces blank. Sometimes they can be heard whimpering at night. This lore is colorful, interesting, scary, and spiritu-al. A collection from Martinique for interested adult story readers is Pat-rick Chamoiseau's *Creole Folktales* (New York: The New Press, 1994). To master telling these tales, one must master the French patois.

AMERICA'S TRIBAL NATIONS

Tribal nations of America believe the story *itself* has power when told at powwows, rituals, and ceremonies. Relevant to discussions of storytell-ing in America's tribal nations is the following quote:

> The great majority of Europeans who crossed the Atlantic in the early stages of the colonization of the Americas, whether driven by quest for religious liberty for themselves or by visions of opportunities for riches or material success in "new-found" America carried their old ethnocen-tric prejudices with them. Equating civilization and culture with Eu-rope and its modes of expression and lifestyles, they were stricken by New World cultural blindness and consequently failed to "discover" the significance, spiritual and esthetic values, and beauty of the unique and antique literature of the original Americans.[5]

Stories from America's tribal nations reflect group experiences and be-liefs. Similar to African traditions, history of the tribes was recorded in stories. Unabashedly accompanied by dance or performance, stories were often ritualistic and sacred. Although similarities may be apparent, each tribe's own stories explained origins of the universe, the earth, and hu-mans. In many narratives, humans were intertwined with the earth and with relationships to animals from which sustenance was gained.

LATIN AMERICA

The term *Latin America* represents many nations and cultures, some with roots on different continents. *Latin America* is used repeatedly but must be considered nondefinitive for the storyteller. Stories from one locality, center, or place must be introduced as from *that* place or region and as representing only one among many concepts. Language and history are the two main coordinating factors for Latin Americans. John Bierhost writes, "Latino folklore is two things at once. For the most part it is distinctly Old World, preserving medieval and even ancient types. And yet in part it is new. That is, it has been enhanced by Indo-America, which retains its own distinctive traditions while contributing a new, mixed lore of European and native elements."[6]

Asbel Lopez, who has written articles about Latin American storytelling, reports that the continent's narrative traditions are a very rich mingling of three historically oral societies: the indigenous Indian; the African; and, to a lesser extent, the local Spanish.

HAWAIIAN ISLANDS

Today, ancient religions may not be practiced in Hawaii and other islands of the Pacific, but stories record some of the old practices and beliefs. Classic tales relate to nature, surrounding jungles, volcanoes, hurricanes, floods, oceans, and water adventures. The goddess Pele is familiar to peoples around the world. With the influx of nonindigenous cultures, much Hawaiian lore became relegated to the past until concerned, cultural leaders began a movement of revival. Currently, early narratives appear more readily in print. Stories from Hawaiian culture are adopted by other cultures on the islands, but changes can often be identified by the foods, clothing, and other cultural imprints.

THE ORIGIN OF STORIES

A Seneca legend presents Poyeshao[n] (Orphan), who is the first of his tribe to discover stories told to him by the stone. In the end, the stone says, "I have finished! You must keep these stories, as long as the world lasts; tell them to your children and generation after generation."[7]

The Ekoi people of Africa surmised that because Mouse went everywhere—to the houses of the rich and the poor—she was able to weave story children of all types, wearing gowns of various colors. The story children lived in Mouse's house, and when a fight ensued between the Nimm woman and Sheep, Mouse's door accidently opened and stories ran out all over the earth. They never returned but still continue to run everywhere in the world.

"How Spider Obtained the Sky God's Stories"[8] is an Ashanti tale told in a popular picture book titled *A Story, a Story*.[9] The same story, having slight variations, is found in several collections of African folktales. Anansi the spider is able to accomplish feats that so impress the Sky God and the elders that they give or sell him the coveted box of stories. Anansi becomes owner of all the stories, formerly property of Onyankopon, the Sky God. In one version, the python is the first to be captured by Anansi, while in *A Story, a Story*, the first to be captured is Osebo, the leopard with the terrible teeth. The other missions to be accomplished by the spider-man are the same: to capture Mmboro and the hornets and to bring Moatia the fairy to the sky god. In the end, all stories become Anansi stories.

An Inuit myth tells how a young man, Teriak, brought back from the eagle people the greatest gift of all, the gift of joy. The eagles taught Teriak how to hold a song festival, and now it is the duty of human beings to sing and to be happy—their joyful sounds will rise up from earth to make old eagles young again.[10]

Contrast these myths and folklore to Brian Boyd's *On the Origin of Stories*.[11] He contends that because social beings need to communicate with each other, humans are hard wired to tell stories. Why we listen to and tell stories that are imaginative is questioned and explained. Boyd theorizes that humans need play and with play comes creativity. Stories provide imaginative play, arousing our emotions and imprinting our memories with lasting metaphors. He further suggests that story play is comparable to the interface between art, real stories, and drama. Because all arts are made more compelling by the act of storytelling, participation in and appreciation of story art are necessary for successful human development, Boyd proposes.

Information from musicologists and art historians offer theories of ancient developments that appear to support Boyd's theories about the interweaving of music, paintings and sculptures, and narrative arts. Examine the following statements:

- [On ancient Chinese music] Music played an important part in Chinese secular life, too. Just as feudal lords of the Middle Ages received minstrels and troubadours into their castles to entertain them, so the Chinese princes and potentates hired jesters, dancers, epic poets, musicians and puppet theatre groups. Throughout the ages these performers kept alive the *rich treasury of legends* and traditional arts of the distant past.[12]
- [On Chinese shadow puppets] The Chinese narrative tradition does not always require such an elaborate setting. In addition to many kinds of small theatricals there is a lovely shadow puppet tradition that uses a small ensemble of opera instruments backstage to accompany the narrator-manipulator. There are at least two major

traditions of solo narrators. The first sometimes called *tan tz ' u . . . .* The other narrative tradition is called *ta ku tz ' u . . . musical storytelling* as such has belonged since at least the Sung dynasty to the itinerant street musician whose appeal was to the peasant and passerby.[13]

- [On music cultures] Another important feature of Central Asian music is the presence of *long-epic narratives*. It is from traditionally unaccompanied songs of their *storytellers* that many folk epics of this area have been recovered.[14]
- [On early Japanese narrative and theatrical traditions] During the twelfth and thirteenth centuries a tradition arose called *heike-hiwa* in which a famous *war narration* was sung to the accompaniment of a hiwa lute. The music consisted of lines of poetry chanted to named stereotyped melodies. . . . Many of the names of both the vocal and instrumental patterns were derived from Buddhist chant nomenclature. This style of narration became very popular and though *heike-hiwa* itself is practically extinct today, its tradition is carried on in a similar, if more flamboyant, style by modern hiwa and shamisen narrators.[15]
- ["On Dancing Girl and Musicians" (wall painting), Ajanta Caves, India, sixth century AD] The whole wall-painting illustrates the Mahajanaka Jataka *(a story from the Jataka, the tales of the previous incarnations of the Buddha)* which tells of a man marked out to attain wisdom.[16]

As people have traveled, so have stories, intertwined and updated by place and time. Accordingly, the roots of early narratives are hard to trace. Historians, folklorists, scientists, and philosophers documented, codified, and interpreted early records, providing historical and biological explanations of human development. With thorough investigations, theories, and examinations of data, much of this information became early science. Around the world, archaeologists continue to uncover more historical developments. Each bone; shard of pottery; remnant of clothing; and writing on walls, cloth, or papyrus brings revision to evolving stories. Retellings appear after each discovery.

Periodically, stories and storytelling seem to disappear into the "mist of time." Advances in space travel; development of powerful telescopes, satellites, and robots in space; and discoveries of new planets have altered astronomy and space science. However, instead of diminishing humanity's awe and wonder, expansion into the universe's frontiers has fueled further quests for discovery. In reverence for the *heavens* the eternal question remains, Why?

CULTURE

For anthropologists who study the development of cultures and analyze local developments, a standard component of their research is the study of existing stories. Showing dedication to their findings, Harold Courlander, Roger Abraham, and James Campbell, all anthropologists and folklore specialists, have become collectors of stories. These noted folklorists agree that much of culture is rooted in the story.

Storytelling assisted in establishing central relationships among people, delineating family roles, developing rules for social organizations, anchoring religious rituals, and eventually building institutions. East, west, south, and north, stories were told before they were recorded.

Polygenesis, the spontaneous creation of the same story by different peoples in different places, is a widely accepted thesis. Author and researcher in this genre Joseph Campbell suggests that stories with the same basic theme appear all over the world partly as evidence that tales were told long before being written down. He supports the belief that the same tales and motifs are found in many cultures because people are the same everywhere, having the same questions and wonder about their universe and humanity. Others contend that tales originated in each culture from which they came. One argument is that polygenesis may be too often used as the basis for human "sameness" and that the existence of folktales sharing the same patterns may have resulted from geography and travel, not polygenesis. Despite universal features, meanings, themes, genres, and styles of storytelling found around the world, particulars of narratives differ from culture to culture.

Features of traditional culture have been lost when whole continents like Africa or South America are seen as a monolith. In Africa, Asia, and South America, as in Europe, storytelling differs across the boundaries of country. Upon examination, plots may have familiar metaphors, while others remain fraught with strange and compelling differences.

Personal Note: A story form the Yoruba people that I tell is "Tintinyin and the Unknown King of the Spirit World."[17] Although in much more detail, the metaphors of the story are reminders of well-known parables. The following is a synopsis:

> Long ago, a boy called Tintinyin was orphaned. When he was a small child, his father died, and his mother followed his father a few years later. The boy was uncared for and survived in the bush alone with the animals and birds that cared for him, clothed him, and fed him. He learned to understand the language of the animals. Not far from the bush where he lived, there was a large town ruled by an Oba. It had always been said that the king of the Spirit World attended the festival held there, but he was always unseen. Nobody could recognize him. The Oba became anxious to prove this matter, and just before the annual festival, he asked his bellman to announce that anyone who could point out the "king" would receive valuable gifts and be given a high position.

> When Tintinyin heard the message, he went straight to the Oba's palace and de-
> clared that he could identify the king of the Spirit World. On the day of the festival, all
> eyes were on Tintinyin because word had spread about his promise. The Oba called
> the boy to his side, asking him to keep his promise and reminding him that he would
> die if he failed. Since the time he made the promise, Tintinyin had become worried,
> for he had hoped the birds and animals would give him the answer, but none of his
> conversations had produced results. Just as he began to despair, he saw an ega bird
> who spoke to him, telling him how foolish he had been to make such a promise, but
> not wanting to see the boy die, he gave him the answer. He pointed to an old man in
> the crowd, standing and leaning on a stick, and said, "That is the king of the Spirit
> World, and I am your father." Oba now knew it was his father who had given him the
> secret. Tintinyin brought the stranger before the Oba, but the man spoke no words.
> Instead, he pulled up his garment and showed on one leg a tiny bead tied to his
> ankle. This was the symbol of the king of the world of spirits. The old man then
> vanished from sight. The Oba kept his promise, giving Tintinyin valuable gifts and a
> position of stature. Tintinyin became rich and much respected. The Oba never asked
> to see the king of the Spirit World again, but people still say that when he appears
> again, it will be in the clothes of the poor.

In ancient communities invaded by religious or political zealots, existing
stories were destroyed to reduce the influence on new teachings. Appar-
ently, this was especially true in Latin America. To more fully understand lore originating in such places, stories must be studied in the context of the culture.

Intermittent language may become an important factor when words
reflect innuendos of culture. One word or simple phrase may contain
powerful implications. The witch or sorceress of European origin may
become a *cuandera* in a Mexican tale or a *conjur woman* in an African
American tale. Sometimes the supporting culture for a story is observable
by the vocabulary. Entire stories become culturally embodied in one very
culturally specific character or word. *High John, the Conquerer*, appears in
African American tales, while *Ti Jean* shows up in the Caribbean. African
collections also include uniquely plotted dilemma tales, giving the listener a choice of endings. These tales are designed to initiate discussion
rather than offer the usual conclusions with which we are familiar in the
western world. Every culture and culture within cultures has storytelling
shaped by the people of the community. Stories are used for entertainment, for teaching, and for passing on knowledge and wisdom.

Unique specialties and patterns arising within a larger sphere add to
cultural complexities. Because of physical, geographical, or social isola-
tion, specific subcultural patterns are evident in the stories. Such a spe-
cialty would exist in Appalachian tales spawned by communities in the
beautiful, isolated Appalachian Mountains. Mennonites, as only one example of less-dominant religions with longevity, have produced their
own lore. Africans, torn away from their original cultures and carried to
other lands, retained only bits and pieces of their African *roots*. Stories

were devised that reflected their lives of bondage in America, Cuba, Portugal, and other places. A complex set of literature evolved out of the hopes and dreams of these people. Such literature, altered by each place and time, has slowly become mainstreamed in world literature, but many written and recorded narratives remain hidden. Over time, stories of the trickster were popularized, retaining African influence. Original heroes produced for mental and physical survival within the brutal system of slavery are being more widely promulgated.

Personal Note: I have found that few audiences have heard of Peg Leg Joe, a familiar character in some African American communities. The legend relates to slavery and the African American spiritual "Follow the Drinking Gourd." Joe, once a sailor, at times could be seen walking from one plantation to another. Nobody bothered him, but each spring after his visits, hundreds of slaves would disappear. He had taught them how to follow the North Star to freedom.

Often, the story form gives voice to authors, playwrights, and even historians, such as Van Loon, author of *The Story of Mankind*. Written in the early twentieth century, this acclaimed title presents the entire history of Western civilization in a story form considered palatable for children.

Through each millennium, the composite of early literary works have survived. People continue to be empowered by stories that encourage response to the challenges of life and facilitate moving forward with educated choices. The traditional telling of tales continues after having gone through many upheavals. With the rising influence and use of technology, all cultural and performing arts are transforming. In part, storytelling has become replaced by video, radio, and other forms of media. Adults and children have few opportunities to experience person-to-audience story sharing. Indications are that stories will continue to find voice through parents, grandparents, and teachers. Support for storytelling among librarians, once the strongest advocates, has waned but not disappeared. Skilled storytellers may find a place for their voice on the World Wide Web. Long-term purveyors, of storytelling such as the National Storytelling Festival held yearly in Jonesville, Tennessee, spark enthusiasm and produce recruits to the continuance of this tradition. Radio has become a source for story sharing with several popular programs, such as *The Story* originating from North Carolina and *Moth* out of New York. The missions and techniques may not be traditional, but the importance and effect of telling our stories are emphasized. Thus, storytelling, an ancient art, as ancient as the ability to communicate, becomes basic to human culture and remains a living art.

REFERENCES

Bender, Mark. *Plum and Bamboo: China's Suzhou Chantefable Tradition* (Urbana: University of Illinois Press, 2003).

Campbell, Joseph, with Bill Moyers. *The Power of the Myth* (New York: Bantam, Doubleday, Dell, 1991).

Lopez, Asbel. "Weaving Magic with the Unspoken Word," *UNESCO Courier*, May 2001, 54:5, p. 41.

Philip, Neil. *Mythology of the World* (New York: Kingfisher, 2004)

NOTES

1. From the Amazulu, "Unkulunkulu," in *African Myths and Legends*, by Susan Feldmann (New York: Dell, 1963), p. 59.

2. Richard Gray, "Fairy Tales Have Ancient Origin," *The Telegraph*, September 2009.

3. Gray, "Fairy Tales Have Ancient Origin."

4. Anne Pellowski, introduction to *Fourteen Hundred Cowries and Other African Tales*, collected by Abayomi Fuja (New York: Washington Square Press, 1973), p. 9.

5. Abraham Chapman, ed., *Literature of the American Indians: Views and Interpretations* (New York: New American Library, 1975), p. 1.

6. John Bierhorst, *Latin American Folktales: Stories from Hispanic and Indian Traditions* (New York: Pantheon, 2002), p. xi.

7. "The Origin of Stories, a Seneca Legend" in *Literature of the American Indians: Views and Interpretations*, edited by Abraham Chapman (New York: New American Library, 1975), pp. 25–29.

8. "How Spider Obtained the Sky God's Stories," in *African Myths and Legends*, by Susan Feldmann (New York: Dell, 1963), pp. 129–31.

9. Gail E. Haley, *A Story, A Story* (New York: Simon and Schuster [Aladdin], 1988).

10. Neil Phillip, *Mythology of the World* (Boston, MA: Kingfisher, 2004), p. 15.

11. Brian Boyd, *On the Origin of Stories*, (Cambridge, MA: Harvard University, Belknap Press, 2010).

12. Romain Goldron, *Ancient and Oriental Music* (New York: H. S. Stuttman, 1968), p. 67.

13. William P. Malm, *Music Cultures of the Pacific, the Near East, and Asia* (Englewood Cliffs, NJ: Prentice Hall, 1967), p. 12.

14. Malm, *Music Cultures*, p. 65.

15. Malm, *Music Cultures*, p. 141.

16. Sponsored by World Federation of Organizations of the Teaching Profession and UNESCO, *Man through His Art*, vol. 2 (Greenwich, CT: New York Graphic Society, 1964), p. 22.

17. Abayomi Fuja, *Fourteen Cowries and Other African Tales* (New York: Washington Square Press, 1973), pp. 122–37.

TWO
Folklore Defined

> We tend to think of folktales as the purest of fictions, so self-contained and logical in development that they are lit from within and need no explanation. . . . Stories operate like proverbs, as a means of depersonalizing, of universalizing, by couching the description of how specific people are acting in terms of how people have always acted. This is the element of storytelling that we who read books and live in cities tend to discard and forget—the farther away from the village and the oral world we go, the farther behind we leave it.—Roger Abrahams[1]

There is no definition of storytelling covering all of its manifestations in the world, but serious attempts have been made to categorize stories. Those demarcations vary from simple categories, such as family stories, cultural stories, and personal stories, to extensive examinations of narratives called folklore. The word *folklore* was coined by William J. Thomas, a British antiquarian, and may be defined as the traditional beliefs, legends, customs, and more of people and the study of such materials, or the unwritten literature of a people as expressed in folktales, proverbs, riddles, songs, and more. Lore is attached to a particular place and transmitted by the folk orally, while folklore refers to both oral and literary concepts and to a formal set of academic studies. Academically, folklore is the discipline that concerns itself with systematically delineating aspects of culture and social life through studying the existing information about and from the people. Stories or tales in this discipline do not represent entertainment but are sources of information defining the life of various peoples.

Virginia Hamilton introduces tales told in her inimitable way by stating, "Folktales take us back to the very beginning of people's lives, to their hopes and their defeats. . . . Remember that these folktales were once a creative way for an oppressed people to express their fears and hopes to one another."[2] A folktale is a popular story passed on in spoken form from one generation to the next. Usually, the author is unknown, and there are often many versions of the tale. Comprised of fables, fairy tales, old legends, and even "urban legends," selected stories may have transmitted partially hidden truths lost over time. Usually driven by plot more than characters and their actions, folk stories are narrative units with unity and circumscription, distinguishing them from other written forms. Action and conflict move what is usually a simple plot. Conflicts are quickly resolved, and simple conclusions are drawn. Myths, legends, and folktales are hard to classify and often overlap. Symbols of events become more important than the facts. Sometimes, the story takes on a life of its own, entirely eliminating the facts and leaving only the message.

In spoken form, the place or setting of folktales is not known but begins, "Once upon a time" in a forest, a faraway place, or in the country or city. Places of origin may be described in universal terms—European tales often take place in castles of medieval times or in the abode/cottage of a peasant. Similarly, Chinese and other Asian tales frequently are placed in great palaces or in the humble homes of the poor. Usually, only brief notes about setting tie the story to a given culture.

Characters are simple and highly stereotypical. A beautiful princess, a handsome prince, a mean stepmother, the youngest child, the first daughter, the wicked witch, the thief, the clever one, the downtrodden, the peasant, the poor, and the orphan are common. Occasionally, characterizations focus on benevolent or greedy/rich. Physical appearance may not be completely detailed, and usually all descriptions are short.

Plot patterns may be repeated from story to story, with different characters and problems to solve. Solutions to problems may come from supernatural forces, but supernatural creatures are most common to fables and fairy tales. Infrequently, exquisite details illuminate the telling. Modern versions of folk stories, especially those of European derivation, have been designed to end happily, but characters who die or story endings that are fatal appear quite frequently in Latin American and African stories. Hans Christian Andersen's tales, placed in the *literary fairy tale* category, present popular characters meeting deadly fates. *The Steadfast Tin Soldier* and *Little Match Girl* are examples.

Themes of all folktales center on the human circumstance. When these stories were first written for adults or the whole community, they delved into problems of emotions, marital relationships, community relations, and all human encounters with the world. The Grimm brothers are given credit for having been the first to collect tales of the folk in written form. *Kinder und Hausmarchen* was published in three volumes in the seventeenth century. Many revisions have appeared since that time. New, revised versions center on the same problems but focus on appeal to children. There is speculation that the earliest themes are at the very heart of being a child, of adolescent growth, and of learning to be an adult.

Literary style in folktales is recognizably simple and constantly duplicated. Codes or symbols to be remembered by the listener inhabit stories. The magic lamp, the glass slipper, and the magic pot are familiar by repetition. Common motifs are journeys through dark forests, encounters with helpful or dangerous animals, meeting a mysterious person or creature, and accomplishing impossible tasks. Presentation of powerful, memorable images designed to startle or intrigue the listener is common. Envision Rapunzel's hair, the giant beanstalk, the gingerbread house, and other icons. The most effective stories recorded may be those that read as narrations almost begging to be told.

Commonly, there is agreement about the delineations of story categories, with recognition of the many recapitulations and combinations of motifs, which can prove confusing. Categorized by continents, countries, or regions from which they come, folklore collections attempt to place stories in their cultural base.

It seems natural that stories of the *folk* are hard to classify. The continuum and nature of the story form is such that processes for codifying different types of stories and placing them culturally must be difficult. Indexes of tales by Stith Thompson are frequently used, but those also reveal many entanglements. Perhaps, the minor facts, symbols, emotional reactions of the characters, and conclusions drawn are in the end most important. The following are descriptive introductions to selected story forms, simplified for the storyteller.

FABLES

Most often told with animal characters, all fables have moral conclusions. Almost everyone is familiar with at least one of these, even if the source is forgotten. As suggested earlier, the lines are fuzzy regarding countries of origin. Aesop's fables have been placed in Greece, although some believe the writer came from Egypt or North Africa. The preponderance of opinions support, as historical fact, that Aesop's fables (*Aesop* meaning "black" in Greek) were gathered in Greece by a slave living sometime in the sixth century BC. Others argue that credit for these fables should be assigned to Demetrius of Phaleron. Whatever the source, these short tales ending with a moral statement have become staples in literature and in the repertoires of many storytellers. Another major source of fables, differing somewhat from those of Aesop in philosophical content, is the Panchatantra, existing since approximately 200 BC. Some recognizable titles from these two sources are "The Wind and the Sun"; "A Lion and a Mouse"; "The Shepherd's Boy and Wolf"; "The Town Mouse and the Country Mouse"; "The Goose and the Golden Eggs"; "The Fox and the

Grapes"; "The Golden Goose"; and "The Tiger, the Brahman, and the Jackal."

When examining stories from the tribal nations of America and Africa, it is evident why establishment of demarcations between various story types becomes problematic. Use of animals as main characters and purveyors of a message is common in these cultures. Thinly drawn lines make it difficult to determine which of these may be called fables, except for the limiting definition that fables are presented, primarily, for a moral purpose. Adding to storyline complications, offerings called "modern fables" written by storytellers and such folklorists as James Thurber must be given consideration. "Chante-fables" refers, simply, to any story in which a chant, incantation, or song is a major part.

FAIRY TALES

Characters of these stories are elves, hobgoblins, dragons, fairies, and other magical creatures, sometimes interacting with humans or intervening in human affairs. Because some tales have no fairies as characters, it is mainly the magical elements that distinguish them as a category. Fairy tales without fairies take place in an unreal world. These tales seem to speak a language that has resonance with children, assisting many in expressing and reconciling difficult emotions. Possibly because of their innocence, children think in metaphor more than adults.

The messages or morals are similar to other types of tales. Contrary to some opinions, fairy tales did not always have happy endings. Altered for modern audiences, many of the original tales of Grimm had endings that could be considered gruesome. At the end of early versions of "Little Red Riding Hood," the little girl is eaten by the wolf, and that is the last of her. For some cultures, the fairy may not be a charitable character but can be mean and vindictive.

Two thought-provoking essays about adult attitudes toward folk- and fairy tales are found in a respected collection of essays titled *Only Connect: Readings on Children's Literature*. The first is the essay "Children and Fairy Stories" by J. R. R. Tolkien, suggesting that enjoyment of fairy tales may be dependent on the suspension of disbelief, a factor available to children and adults. Another element for acceptance is inner "desire." Tolkien writes, "In my opinion fairy tales should not be specially associated with children. . . . If a fairy story is a kind worth reading at all it is worthy to be written for and read to adults. They will of course put more in and get more out than children can."[3]

Another essay, "The Truth of Fables" by Michael Hornyansky, questions why children were still fascinated with classic fairy stories in modern times (1969). After indications that his own children had a wide range of interests, he declares, "The stories they remember well enough to tell us . . . are Sleeping Beauty, Red Riding Hood, Cinderella, Snow White, Jack in the Beanstalk and that crowd."[4] Hornyansky further proposes that the answer to his question does not lie in an escape from reality, "but quite the contrary, that they [fairy tales] do accurately reflect the child's picture of himself and his family. The father is the king, mother is queen in this tiny world, and they ought to be wise and strong."[5] His contention is that modern stories are further from the child's view of life and compares the child to the dwarf contending with the giant, an adult. He argues that the antagonisms between characters accurately represent a child's emotional quandaries and asks, "Shall we say, for instance, that these classic fairy tales for children are in fact not children's stories at all but folktales from the half-conscious wisdom of the race, expressing in mythic form certain enduring truths?"[6]

LITERARY FAIRY TALE

Literary fairy tales include tales such as those told by Hans Christian Andersen in which humans and inanimate characters hold some of the same powers as fairies. These are tales definitely assigned to an individual author rather than existing in the milieu of the folktale.

MYTHS

Myths could possibly demand a category outside of the sphere of folklore. These stories may be the most revealing of cultural and historical progress among human groups. Ancient people invented gods, shaping them as they wished, larger than the beasts around them and, as would be expected, larger than themselves. After forming these gods in mind and story, they worshipped them regularly. Some expert folklorists propose that mythical gods reflect the social state of the communities who devised them and became their worshippers.

Greek and Norse myths are most familiar probably because these were the first to be formally recorded. Research now provides records of vast oral traditions and views of worldwide mythology. From myths and legends, language and characters have been adopted as part of active communication, especially in western culture. The mythical Cupid symbolizes love, and Psyche refers to the self or the soul. Names of planets and astrological constellations are those of mythical characters. Conceivably, all lore generated from the cultural experience of a people becomes a part of their inner reality. Out of mythical memories come rituals and beliefs.

Historically, among the Inuit people, formal, institutionalized, religious practices were not evident, but there were strong beliefs in the spirit world. This world existed in and about human beings, animals, and the earth. Elements of *spirits* appear strongly in most cultural myths, including those where religious beliefs have been formally established. In Inuit cultures, ancestral spirits have power equal to that of Greek gods.

LEGENDS

Recording unusual and exceptional happenings, feats, and accomplishments experienced by humans, legends may involve the gods but are not necessarily *about* the gods. These are stories about a person or place based on or imitating someone real. The tales of "King Arthur and the Round Table" would be common examples. Knights and kings of their kind may have existed but not as portrayed in tales. Stories about John Henry, Johnny Appleseed, and Pecos Bill exist somewhere between legends and tall tales. All might have had legendary lives, but the stories told about them are highly exaggerated.

TRICKSTER TALES

Trickster tales are found in many places. Commonly known are spider tales from Africa and the cunning coyote and other animals from the tribal nations of America. Neil Philip, who has written several books about mythology states:

> The Native American tricksters take on various animal and bird forms such as a coyote or raven. Spider Woman is an important goddess of the Native American peoples in the southwest such as the Navajo. She is a helper and teacher of mankind, but she is dangerous and unpredictable, with the power to give and take a life. In the myths of Keres she is known as Thinking Woman, the creator who spun the world from her thoughts.[7]

The trickster represents human nature's penchant toward winning against powerful odds or against superior societal norms. The trickster does not always win but survives to fight again. African tricksters perceive, remember, and study the weaknesses of others and use this knowledge for amusement, self-interest, or escape. Tricksters exist on the peripheries of the social order, creating havoc and disharmony in society and threatening community survival. Characters like Tortoise often project evil forces and bad behaviors against which the human community must contend in order to survive. Such individualistic, nonconformist behavior must be kept in check. In communal performances of African proverbs and folktales, the trickster's bad social behavior is usually punished and the evil forces controlled. Tortoise stories function to reaffirm the priority of wisdom. Communities are reassured that balance and harmony can be restored. Roger Abrahams postulates:

Trickster is the figure who most fully illustrates how not to act within society. But whereas his activities comment implicitly on improper behavior and do it within a fictional form, gossip comments more explicitly and is based on stories purported to be true. In the village environment, gossip is needed to provide everyone with kind of a social map of the terrain.[8]

BALLAD

Primarily with romantic themes, ballads are narrative poems usually formatted in short stanzas and commonly set to music. These narrative folktales in modern form are found in the blues, country music, and even rock and roll. One popular story-ballad especially enjoyed by children is "Frog Went-a-Courting."

CUMULATIVE TALES AND REPETITIVE CUMULATIVE TALES

A favorite with children, these are stories in which the original incident, action, or dialogue repeats, accumulates, and is recounted over and over. There may be lines with a character or phrase added with each repetition. Examples are "The Old Lady Who Swallowed a Fly," "The House That Jack Built," "The Gingerbread Man," and many other modern stories in this form.

RIDDLE TALES

This story form presents a character solving a question posed at the beginning. The riddle solver shows ingenuity and almost godlike qualities. Riddles are inserted in any of the other folktale categories, and a riddle may provide a surprise story ending. One sample is Harold Courlander's "Cow-Tail Switch," in which five sons seek their father, hoping to bring the man home from a fatal hunt. After the details of the adventure and the brothers' special feats, this question is posed: Which brother did the most to bring his father back from the dead?

HERO OR HEROINE TALES

Heroes are characters that are not perfect but have special attributes. They are brave and noble or show exceptional ability. Encompassed in the tales are models or ideals of a given culture. The idea is that some persons are bigger than life. These stories may fit in all the other categories, although for some literary critics, *hero* requires a more detailed definition. Further fracturing of the hero includes romantic hero, superhero, and action hero.

BEAST TALES

In beast tales, unlike other animal tales, creatures are usually dangerous to humans, sometimes pointing to human foibles. Audiences respond favorably to "East of the Sun and West of the Moon" and "Beauty and the Beast," classic beast tales.

MORAL TALES

Sometimes called morality tales, these are narratives that present a moral consequence or serve to convey or teach a moral or moral lesson. Included are fables, proverbs, and other motifs.

DROLL STORIES

These are the tongue-in-cheek stories of blunders, numskulls, and buffoons. The humorous characters exude stupidity and odd behavior. Some "Jack" tales fit into this category as well as "The Three Sillies." Historically, Honoré de Balzac's tales have been considered drolls.

GIANT TALES

Everyone is familiar with stories of characters of superhuman size. They have phenomenal strength and power and are feared by animals and humans.

GHOST STORIES

Stories depicting frightening and imaginative happenings are extremely popular. Children and adults seem to like hearing about supernatural beings, spirits of the dead, and visitations from the dead. Listeners confront superstitions and fears when facing apparitions, strange noises, and other horrors.

ADVENTURE STORIES

An adventure story may portray the exploits of a hero or a group. It can involve exciting explorations or undertakings, usually with dangerous encounters. These heroic tales are exemplified in "The Steadfast Tin Soldier" by Hans Christian Andersen. The one-legged soldier falls from the window and has many adventures before returning to his place of origin and deadly fate.

POURQUOI OR WHY STORIES

The question, Why? is asked and answered in these narratives, which provide simple but intriguing answers to inquiries about the universe and human actions. In answer to the wonders of life and the universe, early shamans, griots, and medicine men shaped these narratives.

NONSENSE TALES

Sometimes in convoluted language, nonsense tales are foolish, exaggerated, or improbable. Edward Lear is the master teller of nonsense tales and creator of nonsense verse. Some of Dr. Seuss's popular stories could be considered nonsense tales. Maurice Sendak's use of nonsense words in *Higglety, Pigglety, Pop* have uncanny appeal for the young. Children respond to the humor and have fun trying out the sounds on their tongue.

FRAME TALES

A tale within a tale, frame tales are often found in novels formatted by an author using cultural myths within a modern story.

REAL STORIES

In the *real* stories about historical figures and events, characters are sometimes made larger than life. It is the added legends that make learning about these historical "giants" appealing to young and old. Travel, discovery, and invention have appeal for some storytellers and may be useful to those facilitating learning through using the narrative. Some authors, such as Virginia Hamilton, show exceptional skill in capturing the truths of history as story. In her title *Many Thousand Gone: African Americans from Slavery to Freedom,* using the story form, she tells the history of slavery, including uprisings; a biography of Frederick Douglass; and much more.

MOTIFS

Thematic and symbolic motifs are recurring themes or ideas in folk- and fairy tales. Repeated themes found over and over in tales from every culture may be evidence of the universal quest for truth in the story.

The use of threes some say originates with the Trinity of Christian origin, which came late in the evolution of the story. As early as in Aesop's fables we find the symbol of three. Stories often give the protagonist three times to solve a riddle and receive the reward, or the main characters are three, as in "The Three Little Pigs," "Goldilocks and the Three Bears" (it was the third bed which was just right), "The Three Billy Goats Gruff," and even Shakespeare's three witches. Threes are used in Greek mythology. The three virtues that accompanied the goddess Venus were games, grace, and the laughs. There are the three heads of the dog Cerberus and the three furies, Alecto, Megere, and Tisiphone. No one seems to be clear on the origin of the phenomena of threes.

Wishes are granted in so many stories, primarily to persons without power. This is a forceful indication that the preponderance of stories arose from peasantry hoping to better their lives. Stories told for higher echelons reversed this process and granted the wishes of kings, queens, and masters.

Magic objects are prevalent in stories. One of the more famous magic objects is Aladdin's lamp in "Arabian Nights." The featured object may be discovered, given to a traveler, or appear out of nowhere. When directions are carefully followed or obeyed, good luck is the usual result, but revenge can occur upon betrayal.

Poor persons become rich, as in Aesop's fable "The Golden Goose," representing the person who becomes rich but is dissatisfied and ruins chances for financial stability. There are very many tales of this type, including "The Fisherman's Wife," who is granted many wishes and will not stop asking for more until she has nothing. The golden goose as a character appears in at least three variations of fable and folktale. In a version from the Panchatantra, the golden goose visits a poor mother and daughter, giving them one of its golden feathers to sell for sustenance. Although the goose promises to return when needed, the greedy mother conspires to take all the feathers. When she does, the feathers are no longer gold. In the Aesop version, a man owns a goose that lays a golden egg every day. Wishing to get rich fast, he kills the goose in search of all the eggs, finding there are none. The morals or messages are much the same as are the stories.

When animals turn into humans or vice versa, do these transformations in folk stories represent reincarnation? In "The Frog Prince," the human trapped in a frog's body is released from enchantment with a kiss from the princess. In "East of the Sun and West of the Moon," the bear (a prince) has been cursed by his stepmother. It is the eventual love of a young girl that saves him.

More often than not in folktales, the youngest child is the smartest or the most clever. "Boots and Brothers" by Grimm is an example of this recurring theme. Almost like a rule of thumb, the most naïve or innocent character is the winner in classic folktales.

Pots become vehicles of magic numerous times and in many places. In an African story "The Pots That Sang," no one can figure out why the pots made by the best village potter become useless because they only dance and sing. What is it that has cast this spell? The pots sing and dance when the potter is away, greatly disturbing the village. The potter decides to stop his trade and farm full time. A neighbor who has always watched and admired the making of the pots takes on the job. The new potter decides one day that he needs a new stick for stirring clay. When he throws the old stick into the lake, the stick sings. It is only then the source of the pots' singing is known. "Stone Soup" is the classic tale of a man who uses his "magic" pot to entice a village to share hidden food and make enough soup for everyone. In "The Talking Pot," the vessel not only runs but steals from the rich and gives to the poor couple who are its owner.

As said in an anthology of children's literature,[9]

> In all tongues and all times since humanity began, the most familiar words of childhood have probably been, "Tell me a story." And stories have been told, not really for children, but for adults. As they always do, children have listened in, beyond the edges of the fire's light, to hear what tales were told. Those they could grasp, they took to themselves, until, over the stretch of centuries, certain stories have become their own. Unfortunately, with the rise of the modern world, grownups have abandoned the folk tales of simpler times and quieter places as fit only for the young. Now folk tales are mainly the province of children and scholars, but surely anyone who knows folk tales will agree with Horace: "Change the name and the tale is about you." The *tale* is all tales humans have ever told: the *you* is all of us.

NOTES

1. Roger D. Abrahams, *African Folktales: Traditional Stories of the Black World* (New York, New York: Pantheon, 1983), pp. 2–3.

2. Virginia Hamilton, *The People Could Fly* (New York: Knopf, 1985), p. ix.

3. J. R. R. Tolkien, "Children and Fairy Stories," in *Only Connect: Readings on Children's Literature*, edited by Shiela Egoff, G. T. Stubbs, and L. F. Ashley (Toronto: Oxford University Press, 1969), p. 114.

4. Michael Hornyansky, "The Truth of Fables," in *Only Connect: Readings on Children's Literature*, edited by Shiela Egoff, G. T. Stubbs, and L. F. Ashley (Toronto: Oxford University Press, 1969), p. 121.

5. Hornyansky, "Truth of Fables," 122.

6. Hornyansky, "Truth of Fables," p. 131.

7. Neil Philip, *Mythology of the World* (New York: Kingfisher, 2004), p. 51.

8. Roger D. Abrahams, *African Folktales* (New York: Pantheon, 1985), p. 23.

9. Quote in *Arbuthnot Anthology of Children's Literature*, 4th ed., by May Hill Arbuthnot and Zena Sutherland (Glenview, IL: Scott, Foresman, 1976), p. 148.

THREE

Educational Value

I always believed that education was a great instrument to rectify the ills of society. —John Hope Franklin [1]

Chapters 1 and 2 establish that storytelling in early times was the major means by which people in a tribe, village, community, or town were instructed. Modern use of the story in education has fluctuated.

Reinforcing the educational value of storytelling in the book *Deep Like the Rivers: Education in the Slave Quarter Community, 1831–1865,* Thomas Webber finds that:

> Through the medium of stories blacks learned of life in Africa, of the nature of slavery in other states, of the existence of the North and Canada, of the history of their home plantation and the happenings on other plantations, and of the deeds and daring of black heroes and folk heroes. Often, it was through stories that slave children learned bits of their family history. [2]

Having little access to books and other materials, the children of slaves learned through observation and by the story. As in most oral cultures, storytelling was the vehicle for education, illustrating theories and formatting heroic models.

Early education in American was influenced by seventeenth-century Puritanism. It was felt that literature appropriate for children was only that which was repressive and which frightened little persons into moral righteousness. This attitude was somewhat challenged by John Locke's *Some Thoughts Concerning Education,* in which he suggests that children could be led to learning through literature. He recommends Aesop's fables but not fairy tales. Puritanical attitudes in Europe and America were gradually affected by the likes of John Newbery, the Brothers Grimm, Charles Perrault, Charles Lutwidge Dodgson, Kenneth Grahame, and Beatrix Potter.

For many years educators accepted storytelling as one of the arts that can contribute to a student's success. In the United States and other western cultures, formal systems of schooling developed using the story as a vehicle for learning at all levels. Early school materials for teachers included rhymes and poetry for recitation, learning and reading aloud fables, traditional stories and Bible stories, real stories and tall tales about famous people, and examining scientific or geographical narratives. Although designed for parents, such titles as *The Child's Treasury*, edited by May Hill and published in 1921, were standard fare for the classroom teacher. This book's table of contents lists "Nursery Rhymes," "Nursery Songs and Illustrations," "Animal Stories" (including some fables), "Classic Tales and Every-Day Stories" (including fairy tales like Cinderella), "Myths and Legends," "Travels in Foreign Lands," "Nature Study," "Character Sketches," "Heroes and Patriots," "Dramatizations," "Poems," and "Prayers and Bible Stories." In the foreword, May Hill writes, "By means of these, the child's curiosity is roused, he is stirred to emulation, his knowledge is broadened and enriched."[3]

Educational value in the use of stories was obviously assumed, but as years passed, few formal studies documented classroom storytelling as an asset. One such study, "Effects of Storytelling: An Ancient Art for Modern Classrooms" (1982), finds that as technology advanced, children were still fascinated with storytelling—someone standing in front of them with no visuals and no books (excluding storytelling with the plentiful array of picture books). They asked for certain stories to be told over and over again. At the time, according to the writers, some teachers and adults found the telling of stories frivolous and silly. But the investigators proclaim:

> Though children delight in stories, classroom storytelling has a raging reputation among school teachers. Some feel telling a story to the class is frivolous, a treat, and even silly. Yet teachers who learn to become storytellers find they enjoy themselves and their classes in a new way. . . . Because storytelling retells and symbolically interprets the simple incidents of life, it seems to fulfill a basic language function for the young child. When you tell a story, you are speaking their language.[4]

Agreeing that, almost instinctively, many experts accepted storytelling as a basic tenet of education, the investigators find little proven evidence exists that storytelling had any particular effect or educational value. Further, they find that it was rare to find a teacher well-versed and experienced in storytelling. The small evaluative pamphlet continues with assessment of an experiment testing effects of storytelling on learning. Recorded are findings from the brief study of "Word Weaving," an exploration of storytelling in the classroom. The Pittsburg, California, School District participated in this experiment in 1981. Trained storytellers were invited to classrooms. Teachers and librarians sometimes combined forces for effectiveness. With some lingering questions and anomalies, the concluding statement of these authors is:

> Regular use of Word Weaving techniques . . . improves children's fluency and imagination when they create a story based on one they hear, and may help them remember and retell stories. The teachers who used word weaving in [this] study unanimously attested to storytelling's benefits on children's oral language development, comprehension, and fundamental understanding of story.[5]

Although teaching is not the primary intention of seasoned storytellers, listeners learn from them. While joyously experiencing a story, any audience finds elements of themselves, religions, cultural views of the world, and other interesting bits of information about lands and peoples. Using the same methodology for telling, a teacher can elaborate specifically for educational purposes. Interested in results more than audience response, educators have the added responsibility of evaluation, making the teacher-storyteller's job more complex.

In a multicultural democracy, acceptance and understanding of group differences is required. Listening to and learning stories reinforce the individual's sense of self while simultaneously providing evidence for intergroup understanding. Cultures and people are not the same, but the human quest for survival has universal likenesses.

Disciples of storytelling propose that many educational advantages result from storytelling. Books on storytelling specifically written for teachers are available. Some prominent theses and arguments regarding the value of the story as an educational tool follow.

DEVELOPS INTEREST IN READING AND IN CLASSIC LITERATURE

Parents, librarians, and teachers alike hope that storytelling will lead listeners to the enjoyment of reading. Good storytelling forms the basis for the best plays, television shows, movies, novels, and short stories. For older children, the teacher-storyteller might select stories from books similar to *Stories from Shakespeare* as an introduction to further study. Within any classic title, there are incidents or brief excerpts worth telling. Instructors for persons training to work directly with children in libraries traditionally include this technique as the substance of "book talks." Anthologies of children's literature generally include such excerpts readymade for the teacher-storyteller's use. An incident involving the main character of any book told as a story invites the students to read or learn more. Selections from literature classics like *Black Beauty* and *Old Yeller* can easily be found.

There is no explanation for children developing such a strong liking for certain stories and story types in their early years, but this penchant toward liking a certain story and another like it continues into adulthood. Selections that will provide that key for one pupil will be rejected by others. Variety is extremely important.

Personal Note: While fulfilling an assignment at the University of Wisconsin, Milwaukee, the high school literature teacher at a school nearby complained to me that his students showed no interest in Shakespeare. He needed strategies for engagement of *inner-city*, predominantly African American, students in learning Shakespeare. After reminding him of books that simplified the frequently complex language of classics, such as *Stories from Shakespeare* by Marchette Chute and *Beautiful Stories from Shakespeare* by Edith Nesbit, I proposed having students read the plays with the intent of rewriting each play and forming their own *story* with a modern theme or slant. If they wished, their creations could be written in local vernacular. After devising a lesson plan using this idea, the teacher reported that students became more interested and involved. One rewritten narrative of *The Taming of the Shrew* was submitted complete with a visiting Avon lady!

Due to fiscal constraints, art and music departments have been deleted from many school budgets. Acting out a story might be a child's first introduction to plays. An interesting article about story theater titled "Full Circle" by Walter Dallas appears in *Jump Up and Say!*, a delightful collection of African and African American lore. He explains,

> Story theater means theater in which the storytelling technique involves an intricate layering of character, ritual, improvisation, time, place, transformation, imagination, motivations and so forth. . . . The cement that holds the stories together is the power in the ability to transform time, object, and character: the ability to become one with the event . . . like a griot who bears witness because he remembers with his feelings and touches with his voice."[6]

The process of creatively building story circles upon circles on stage is fascinating and worthy of investigation by those interested in teaching theater and other creative arts.

Personal Note: Over years of responding to invitations to visit hundreds of classrooms, one of the activities I added to the storytelling was called simply "acting out the story." After hearing the story, this process involved instant improvisation of the characters by the students. For example, in one memorable case, a fourth-grade class was told "The Frog Prince." The story was reenacted several times to give more children a chance to participate. Roles were assigned by the teacher, and characters were added to involve more children. One added character was the butler. It was he who opened the door to let the frog meet the princess. Several humorous responses were created by each butler. When opening the door, one said, "Go away, creep, or you may end up in the soup." Another said, "Ugh, what big eyes you have!" probably remembering the wolf in "Little Red Riding Hood." The teacher and I were most surprised when the person playing the butler opened the door and said, "By Jove! There's a frog out here" with a very good imitation of an English accent. This was a class of inner-city African American children given a much-needed opportunity to fantasize and create. Most poignant were those who wanted desperately to be the handsome prince. When on stage, all one boy said repeatedly was, "I am a handsome prince!"

At another elementary school, with no prompting from me, several teachers joined forces in presenting a stage play of the story "Why the Sun and Moon Live in the Sky." They asked me to return for the showing. The children had drawn backdrops with African patterns and motifs. The teachers (I'm sure with parents' help) had made costumes of colorful African dress. Large handheld masks represented the animals and the sun and moon. It was quite striking as cardboard paintings of water rose higher and higher and the sun and moon climbed higher and higher on the steps of camouflaged ladders.

PROMOTES LEARNING ABOUT EACH OTHER

Stories create memorable sharing experiences, helping participants know each other better or introducing listeners to unfamiliar cultures. There is no doubt that in ways never conceived of when storytelling began, the World Wide Web has made learning about various peoples accessible. But somehow cultural separation continues as a barrier to appreciation and understanding. One causative factor for such alienation may be selective terminology used when referring to or presenting other cultures. Perhaps the use of language like *aliens, primitive, foreign,* and *strange* should be excluded from the vocabulary of teachers, storytellers, and adult interveners who wish to promote cultural understanding. Differences must be affirmed, but terms like *people everywhere, people all over the world, children in many countries* immediately eliminate barriers. Story programs designed to spotlight a selected culture are valid, but presenting selections from several cultures may be most important. Many stories are available to introduce and entice students to study subjects about which they are reluctant to learn.

Personal Note: In the 1970s, as a member of the California Librarians Black Caucus (CLBC), I suggested that our regular program at the California Library Association be different. I proposed a live demonstration of storytelling with inner-city African American children, with the opportunity for librarians to observe the response and effect. The proposal was accepted, and the program was arranged. Hearing of this activity, members of Reforma (the Spanish-speaking caucus of librarians) requested to be partners in this venture. The program was carefully arranged so busloads of children could be brought to the convention center. Rooms were assigned, and a list of storytellers was scheduled. Space for librarians to observe was assigned in the back of each room. The program was a resounding success. During my sessions and reportedly from other librarians, the children were very responsive and well behaved, only wishing they could stay longer. Librarian observers also gave positive responses. Aside from the value of the storytelling experience, this "outing" gave the children a view of a large adult conference, which could be explained to them by teachers. Some classes managed to gain entrance to the exhibit hall and were most pleased to receive publishers' giveaways. One young boy whose face I can still see was lined up with his class, ready to leave the storytelling venue. He tugged at my arm and said, "You were great. So this is how is the rich people live. That sure is a beautiful pool. If they would let me, I'd get in there with my clothes on." He laughed and said goodbye.

HELPS LISTENERS LEARN ABOUT AND APPRECIATE THEIR OWN CULTURAL HERITAGE

Everyone enjoys finding someone like themselves in a story, in a book, or on the screen. People identify with what they know best. This may be one reason some communities retain cultural cohesiveness. A sense of self is important, but in a democracy and increasingly in the global sphere, it becomes dangerous when cultural norms are reasons to reject others who are different. Minority groups are usually pleased when stories about them are told well and when an audience responds positively to stories with which they identify.

Personal Note: More often than not, my storytelling has included some Anansi tales or Br'er Rabbit tales. On several occasions, listeners from Africa and the Caribbean have spoken to me afterward with affirmation. I've been asked, "Are you from Haiti?" "You come from Belize?" "What part of Africa are you from?" It has been a joy to be claimed as "sister" by Haitians, Ghanaians, Nigerians, Cubans, and others.

In 2007, I was invited to be the family "griot" at a reunion of one part of my family on the east coast. When I told stories to several generations, the responses were sometimes surprising. Many told me they had never heard a live storyteller. Others knew little of the family history that I shared through stories, but none, including the youngest, seemed bored.

DEVELOPS LISTENING SKILLS

In a world filled with bits and bytes, attention spans of both children and adults are affected. The concentration needed to absorb a story in its full meaning develops listening skills. Teaching storytelling to students within courses like English, history, or literature can be helpful. Student tellers, having the expectation that others should listen while they are applying effort, concentration, and dedication to communicating a story, begin to appreciate the need to listen.

TRANSMITS ETHICAL VALUES

As already mentioned, many folktales have elements of morals or morality. Individual educators and storytellers must decide with which of these elements they feel comfortable. Many stories can become the catalyst for discussion, especially with older children and adults. Stories fitting almost any moral can easily be found by visiting libraries, searching indexes, or surfing the Internet.

Schools all over the United States have been confronted with such issues as bullying, brutality, lying, and violence. Fables and folklore, especially "moral tales," are available to promote discussions of these topics. A simple example is "The Boy Who Cried Wolf," an Aesop fable in which the shepherd boy cries wolf, knowing he is not being truthful. He is amused when the village responds and comes to his aide. After the lie is repeated several times just for fun, a wolf really does appear. No one pays attention when the boy calls for help, and sheep are killed. In "The Lion and the Mouse," a mighty lion is about to attack and kill a little mouse. The mouse begs for mercy, saying "Maybe I can help you one day." Amused, the lion lets him go. Later, the lion, caught in a trap of ropes, is released by the mouse, who chews through the rope. The lion is forever grateful. The simple moral could certainly be used for a perusal of bullying.

DEVELOPS LANGUAGE AND VOCABULARY

Psychologists indicate that a child's communication begins with cries, body language, and eye contact, but he or she soon becomes verbal by imitation. Young children, in particular, gain language from the sound of words and the introduction of language patterns. This process continues when they begin to read. Older children and adults also discover words from the telling of stories and may gain more vocabulary than they realize. Useful to teachers are story collections that include glossaries of unfamiliar terms. Sometimes, it is *unnecessary* to define longer or more complex words if they become defined by the story itself. Puzzled, listeners will most likely ask or search for the meaning. It seems logical that if second-, third-, and fourth-graders can pronounce the names of dinosaurs, they can deal with complex words.

Personal Note: In a first-grade classroom, I began telling "The Three Billy Goats Gruff" and, after scary encounters with the ogre under the bridge, delivered two goats to safety. As soon as it was announced, "And along came the third billy goat," a little boy in the front row startled me by shouting, "Oh, no! Not another one!" When I briefly paused, he said, "Go on!" When the third goat was safely eating grass, the children joined me in saying, "Snip, snap, snout, this tale's told out!" including that little boy.

Obviously, he had heard the story before but allowed himself to be immersed in emotion. He was aware of the happy ending, as were others, but they all wanted to hear the words, to share the journey, and to *savor the language.*

ENRICHES LEARNING AT ALL LEVELS

Almost every person, upon reflection, can remember one lecture or speaking event, when a bit of a story was told, amplifying and clarifying the speaker's thesis. Sometimes, the story told is the only item later clearly recalled. Myriads of topics to be discussed from fairy or folktales include friendship, love, villains, heroes, messengers, parents, other places (real and unreal), travel, human attributes (physical and emotional), work, endurance, wealth, class and status, earning respect, and the wisdom of the elderly.

Personal Note: When visiting classrooms, I seldom used stories as a means to teach. This was left to the teacher. Some were kind enough to send me the results of their follow-up sessions. As a children's librarian, inevitably my book talks included excerpts from novels and first-person narratives of biographical figures.

   Answering a request for storytelling at a correctional institution for women, it was my deliberate choice to tell stories that would encourage, inspire, and challenge the women to think about their plight through the symbolism of the story. After the first session, the young women participated in a conversation about the meaning of the stories. Later, the counselor asked me to return on the day when the inmates' children were brought to the facility for a visit. Because of positive responses to my first visit, another request was received for storytelling with the children and demonstrations for the mothers on the use of books and storytelling with their children. These were memorable occasions.

The rewards of storytelling can surpass the usual understandings of success. A teacher of educable mentally challenged students asked me to participate in a workshop for teachers exploring the best methods of working with educable students. Students were brought forward to participate in my offering of "Stories with Dance." The story selected was "Anansi and the Bird Man." I told the story as I had usually done with any group, subsequently inviting students to participate in designing their own movements for the characters in the story. There was little hesitancy from this group to get up and try imitating spider movements and bird movements. One child was slow at first to participate but soon began to portray the most beautiful and graceful bird movements. I had observed that child's first chance to choreograph with pleasure. Later, participating in a follow-up discussion with the teachers, I learned that this student had been one of the most difficult with whom to communicate. This demonstration and experience represented a breakthrough for him and his teacher.

Some educational benefits of storytelling may be easy to measure, such as tests of vocabulary improvement, spelling, and knowledge about people and cultures. There are no ways to measure the story impact of the experiences that I have described, but the personal rewards are enormous.

The following are excerpts of letters from educators and students supporting the educational value of storytelling:

- From a junior high school librarian: "From the response of students that day, and their continued enthusiastic references to the occasion, we feel all the more grateful to you. PAY-OLA: Our African folk tales are circulating."
- From an elementary school, 1995: "Your stories introduced our students to the rich oral tradition of Afro-Americans. Your songs and dances delighted and familiarized our students with the rich heritage of African dance and rhythm. . . . Our Afro-American students participated so proudly with their fellow students."
- From an elementary school student in the Library Service Club, 1987: "All of the kids liked your stories, especially when you danced them. There is a boy in our school that is from Figi [*sic*] and he says that they wear the same dress that you wore."
- From a public library report, 1999: "Mrs. Wilkin's programs encouraged families to stay and browse in the library. Parents were interested and asked about the children's collection. Children were interested in reading more folktales."
- From a participant in a workshop on storytelling, 2013 (a mother and two daughters attended): "Thank you so much for taking time to teach and guide us in storytelling. . . . [My daughter] was asked to read at school. The teacher was so impressed, she made [my daughter] come to the front of the class."

NOTES

1. John Hope Franklin (quote) in *A Wealth of Wisdom* ed. by Camille Cosby and Renee Poussaint (New York: Atria Books, National Visionary Leadership Project, 2004), p. 139.

2. Thomas L. Webber, *Deep Like the Rivers: Education in the Slave Quarter Community, 1831–1865* (New York: W. W. Norton, 1978), p. 218.

3. May Hill, foreword to *The Child's Treasury* (Chicago: Foundation Desk Company, 1921), n.p.

4. Catharine Horne Farrell and Denise D. Nessel, "Effects of Storytelling: An Ancient Art for Modern Classrooms" (San Francisco: The Zellerbach Family Fund and The San Francisco Education Fund, 1982), p. 2.

5. Farrell and Nessel, "Effects of Storytelling," p. 21.

6. Walter Dallas, "Full Circle" in *Jump Up and Say! A Collection of Black Storytelling*, edited by Linda Goss and Clay Goss (New York: Simon and Schuster, 1995), pp. 62–63.

II

Developing the Art and Craft

FOUR

The Modern Storyteller

If you look at the world in terms of storytelling, you have first of all, the man who agitates, the man who drums up the people—I call him the drummer. Then you have the warrior who goes forward and fights. But you also have the storyteller who recounts the event, and this is the one who survives, who outlives all the others. It is the storyteller who makes us what we are, who creates history. The storyteller creates the memory that survivors must have otherwise the surviving would have no meaning."—Chinua Achebe[1]

Selected names assigned to storytellers in various cultures include griots, shamans, sages, balladeers, and bards.

WEST AFRICAN GRIOTS

Although very little West African history was inscribed or printed, early travelers and missionaries included written observations in their records. In such reports and descriptions of unfamiliar cultures, the truth was sometimes altered to suit the needs of the writer, but written verification of storytelling as an art in many parts of the African continent was made available. Musician-storytellers known as griots preserved the history of peoples and places in musical chronicles. *Griots and Griottes: Masters of Words and Music* by historian Thomas Hale assigns these bards the elaborate job descriptions of historians, genealogists, advisors, spokespersons, diplomats, mediators, interpreters/translators, musicians/composers, teachers, exhorters, warriors, witnesses, and praise singers. The griot is a living archive of the people's traditions. Fulfilling hereditary expectations these wise bearers of history learned from their parents, who were also griots. Routinely, these artists were called upon to speak for the king or chief, who whispered in the ear of the griot. The translator then delivered the message loudly for all to hear. The arduous task of memorizing births, deaths, marriages, wars, hunts, and clan history was taken seriously. Reportedly, becoming a griot today begins in the family unit, with boys and girls learning from their parents, progressing to a formal griot school and later to an apprenticeship with a master griot. Both boys and girls train to be griots, although griottes may have less freedom to fulfill all the required obligations. Griots of the present draw on the same one-thousand-year-old repertoire of songs. Commonly it is said "When a griot dies, it is akin to a library burning down."

The twenty-one-string kora known as the West African harp is the traditional instrument used to accompany narratives. Skilled griots "speak the kora" (birimingtingo, similar to talking drums). At such gatherings as a wedding, baptism, or child naming, these narrators speak on behalf of each family and provide entertainment. The role of griot remains an integral part of West African culture and has traveled to other parts of the world. Praise songs, narratives, poetry, and spirituals created by African captives in America just prior to the Civil War are linked to these traditions of song and story on the continent.

SHAMANS

This title probably originates linguistically from the Chinese *sha men*, or "Buddhist monk." Shamans, sometimes called "diviners," "medicine men," or "priests," are found in Africa, Australia, North American tribal nations, and many other traditional cultures all over the globe. These persons act as intermediaries between the natural and supernatural worlds, using magic to cure illnesses, foretelling the future, and controlling spiritual forces. They may read omens and interpret the way animals speak. All feats performed support the forces of good. Their dramatic telling of tales is sacred and can sometimes be combined with trances, sacrifices, and prayer. In some areas with strong belief in dreams, shamans refer to such illusions for enlightenment. Ritualistic readings and retellings of lore help communities maintain ties with nature and one another. Male and female positions of shaman are inherited or earned through apprenticeships. Learning and reciting a group's stories, myths, and legends may be demanded for ceremonial rites of initiation.

In tribal nations, an elder tribal historian, male or female, often assumes the familiar storyteller's role. A recent article in *Deseret News* describes the return of human bones from the Smithsonian to tribal lands near the northern Utah border. The bones were those of four Shoshone villagers killed in a massacre. The entire local tribe, members of the Church of Latter-day Saints, chose burial ceremonies reenacting early traditions. The news item reports:

Timbimboo-Madsen, one of about fifty full-blooded Northwestern Shoshone native Americans living in Utah, said she can trace her tribal
lines to the late 1770s. She is reported to have said, Shoshone people
gather each year to "share old stories and encounter new relatives. . . .
Remembrance of those who have passed on allows us to tell their stories and hold onto their ideals because they were good ideals. . . . They
held a real importance of family. . . . Everyone had their place in their
family."[2]

SAGES

Descriptions of sages may seem the least applicable to the modern role of
storyteller. The term is widely found in religious circles referring to those
who passed on the "wisdom of the ages." The three wise men of the Bible
are often called "the three sages." William Shakespeare is known as both
bard and sage. Twenty-first-century storytellers develop wisdom as they
share with audiences of all varieties. Most important, the storyteller
learns from stories they commit to memory and tell. In fact, they may
listen to and study more stories than they will ever tell. Though their
purpose is not to pontificate, the stories told contain phrases and wisdom
from the sages of the past and present. A woman from Johns Island,
South Carolina, is quoted sharing her raw wisdom in the lilting language
of *gullah* influence:

> I tell you, young people got a lot chance to think more in their age than
> I had to think in my days, 'cause I couldn't think 'bout nothing but
> plant peas and corn in my days. But now these children got so much
> different thing to go through and learn, and they got nice schools. If
> they don't learn, it's nobody's fault but their own. Then I try to teach
> them these stories and different song and let them know what blues
> was like in my days coming up. My children like it. They sit down and
> they want me to talk about the past. They enjoy hearing it. I want them
> to know about it, so when I gone there be somebody to carry it on.[3]

BALLADEERS

The tradition of balladeer was found in Great Britain six to seven centuries ago. The ballad singer is sometimes called a bard, musician-poet, or
troubadour. As is true of folktales, ballads were passed on by word of
mouth. Some ballads were sung, but later, literary ballads appeared that
were meant to be read or told. All, including those told, were meant to be
shared rhythmically. Most often they include short verses that rhyme.
The balladeer's stories are sometimes appropriate for children, but many
are epics of history and myth better understood by adults. Themes in a
ballad may be general or culturally specific, covering numerous subjects.

Although balladeers are often equated with troubadours of French tradition, the troubadour is said to have concentrated on stories and songs of love. While discussing myths, Joseph Campbell gives troubadours credit for initiating the romantic definition of love in one of the series of television conversations with Bill Moyers.

Present-day storytellers combine ballads with other narrative types in many of their presentations. Lewis Carroll's "The Walrus and the Carpenter" remains popular, as does Longfellow's "Paul Revere's Ride."

BARDS

One of an ancient Celtic or mystical poets who composed and recited verses celebrating the legendary exploits of chiefs and heroes is a bard. The word is derived from the Celtic *baird* or Irish *bard*. The medieval bard was a professional singer, presenting verses in honor of heroic achievements by princes and brave men. The original legends of King Arthur were told by medieval bards. At least three types of ballads have been found: those celebrating victories with hymns and praise, verses translating laws of the culture, and those delineating family histories. As in previous categories of griots and shamans, bards may have inherited their positions. Largely replaced by troubadours and minstrels who flourished during the Middle Ages, bards lost popularity. These two newer types of performer inherited some functions of the bard, however it bears repeating that troubadours dealt mostly with chivalry and courtly love.

William Shakespeare is known as the "Bard of Avon," having been appropriated the title in recognition of his major contributions, and hence the original meaning of *bard* may have been lost to visions of great writers. The term is prevalent in Ireland and Wales but elsewhere may be used to loosely apply to all poets. A few professional storytellers refer to *themselves* as bards.

Recognizing that storytelling includes writers, poets, and performing artists who create stories, the concentration here is on the person who stands before an audience, sharing narratives and lore that has been retained in their memory. Storytellers present a fine and beautiful art. When performing well, these expert communicators can cut across age and social barriers, but when poorly prepared, the results can be painful. In *Crash Course in Storytelling* by Kendall Haven and Mary Gay Ducey, it is suggested that there are three categories of storytellers: the informal teller, the community teller, and the professional. Noted storyteller Anne Pellowski encompasses much in her definition of *storytelling*: "The entire context of a moment when oral narration of stories in verse and/or prose is performed or led by one person before a live audience; the narration may be spoken, chanted or sung, with or without, musical, pictorial and/

or other accompaniment, and may be learned from oral, printed or mechanically recorded sources."[4]

For those participating in the art of story sharing, there are no hard and fast rules. People create, tell, and live in stories. Sometimes they become the story. Storytellers are not always interested in presenting fantasy versus reality but strive to promote awareness of the "inner self." Primarily, the job of the storyteller is communicating to an audience the essences of joy, sorrow, love, and wonder. A good storyteller establishes an emotional connection with listeners. They know the story; it is not read and is not memorized word for word but is recreated every time it's told. Using primarily the tones and sounds of their voices, these artists take listeners on a creatively designed journey. The teller, concerned with building an intellectual, emotional, and spiritual connection with a group of people, learns to vividly express thoughts and feelings through oral language.

Personal Note: To eradicate the mystery surrounding the storyteller, in my classes and workshops, students are asked, "Has a storyteller been an important factor in your life?" One library school student wrote a required paper on Garrison Keillor of the radio show *Prairie Home Companion*. Keillor was called a "storyteller, whose tales touch your own life." The student's affinity for Keillor came from the feeling that he had shared in the life of the teller. The student wrote, "His stories often come to unhappy or inconclusive ends, or no ends at all. But they are the folk tales of our times, reflecting our wishes, needs and fears. We are too cynical to believe in 'happily ever after.' It is sufficient that we know that we're not alone in our fears."[5]

Storytellers provide personal connections to human history. Ron Jones in *The Tar Heel Junior Historian* writes,

> Storytelling is deeply rooted in the history and people of our state [North Carolina]. The Jack tales and Grandfather tales of the Appalachian Mountains are recounted versions of folk tales and fairy tales that the early settlers brought from Europe. Pirate stories, tales of shipwrecks, and mysteries of the sea paint a vivid and sometimes hostile picture of life along the coast of early North Carolina. African Americans kept alive the trickster stories and folktales of their homeland through Brer Rabbit and Anansi tales. And the Keepers of the Flame passed on the American Indian myths and legends of the Cherokee and other tribes of the Carolinas."[6]

Jones's article credits teachers and librarians with keeping storytelling alive as television and radio and movies became more prominent forms of entertainment.

Today, we find the tradition of storytelling sporadically flourishing in the United States and any place where talented storytellers remain active. Although courses in storytelling have been dismissed as nonessential in several colleges and universities, prose narration still flourishes. Storytellers perform with varying levels of skills. In time, audiences decide which have the most impact.

ATTRIBUTES OF A STORYTELLER

- Likes a Direct Approach to an Audience: Actors who prefer performing in theater more than on the screen often refer to feelings of being more *in touch* with their audience. This is an advantage available to a storyteller. The teller knows when the attention and interest of their audience has been captured and responds accordingly. This person is able to give the impression of sharing, almost as if they were telling a neighbor about a recent happening. There is no barrier between storyteller and audience. Differences fade as the story comes into focus. Storytelling is *not* an art to be chosen by those who recoil from personal closeness. The best *tellers* communicate in a manner close to personal touch.

- Is Imaginative: In order to stimulate imagination, the teller must *have* imagination. The ability to visualize will transfer to listeners, allowing them to suspend disbelief and travel circuitous routes designed by the story. By bringing alive the inner visions of memory, the storyteller stimulates creative thought. Imagination will also be needed in situations where difficulties arise and impromptu adjustments are required.

- Has Discipline to Choose and Commit to Memory Stories Written Well and with Worthy Content: Spending time in the search of stories is a major job for the storyteller. The stories chosen must have enough substance to demand the time necessary for learning. Thinly drawn narratives without nuances fall flat in the attempt to share. Audiences become aware and edgy when a storyteller presents a story to which they have no commitment. Lack of discipline can lead to untimely and culturally embarrassing choices.

- Learns the Value of Using Voice Modulations for Dramatic Effect: Some action and involuntary gestures are to be expected, and natural "hams" may be actively dramatic. But, a storyteller's emphasis must be placed on using the voice as the major tool for translating emotions and suspense.

- Develops Audience Awareness as Part of the Concentrated Effort of Telling a Story: Such awareness is critical and is a plus of this art compared to others. Readers, consumers, and viewers of paintings, films, and other artistic media usually do not have immediate contact with the creators. Storytellers experience live feedback reflected in facial expressions and eye contact. If an audience becomes distracted or for reasons unknown shows little response, a good storyteller has methods of varying the story and commanding the audience's attention.

- Has That Elusive Quality Called "Presence": Presence is a quality hard to define. It is the ability to say without speaking, "I am here and ready to share." The person with such ability gives the impression of caring and confidence. There is openness and no condescension in their demeanor. Body language is most likely a significant factor in this regard. Something about a person is translated through the way they speak, move, stand, and command attention.
- Respects the Narrative Form and the Power of Words: Storytellers become acquainted with and choose *good* stories to tell, realizing they are painting images in words. As folklore adapted to cultures, storytellers adapt to audiences. There is no desire to denigrate any group or culture. Changing a story is the storyteller's prerogative, but respect is given to the original character of the narrative.
- Draws Awareness to a Story's Characters, Allowing Themselves to Fade into the Background: For this reason a storyteller tries not to be overdramatic, unless the drama is the action of a character in the story. The story is important, not the teller. Memorized affectations draw the listener away from the story, its scenery, and characters and to the mannerisms of the teller.
- Understands Pacing: Pacing applies to the volume and rate of speaking. According to the action, the voice moves slow and fast when necessary. Action mostly moves at a faster pace than dialogue. Pauses for moments of transition are recognized and used effectively.

Nancy Schimmel says,

> We all have stories: stories that are handed down in our families, stories and jokes that we hear and retell with small changes, and stories about things that happen to us. . . . Some of us are professional storytellers, some of us are amateurs, some tell out of choice and some out of necessity, but we are all storytellers, even if the only stories we tell are stories about why we were late this morning. We are all storytellers, but some of us tell stories better, and some of us are better at remembering the right story for the right moment. The skills of choosing, learning and telling stories can be acquired.[7]

Storytellers constantly reshape the world for listeners, challenging their imaginations and yielding innovative thinking. In many ways this intricate art or process involves an incredible exchange of difficult questions and even more difficult answers. The mutual journey made by storyteller and audience is made possible by the muddles, confusions, and changing understandings that exist on both sides of the spectrum.

Provided to emphasize the variety of modern storytellers committed to the art is the following list of professional storytellers listed as they appear in the title *Ready-to-Tell Tales: Sure-Fire Stories from America's Favorite Storytellers.*[8]

- David Novak: Has twice been featured at the National Storytelling Festival
- Carol Birch: Produced an American Library Association (ALA)–notable recording
- Bill Harley: A singer, songwriter, and storyteller
- Len Cabral: Founded Sidewalk Storytellers, a children's theater company
- Judith Black: Has twice been featured at the National Storytelling Festival
- Maggi Kerr Peirce: Born in Ireland; has been a performer at the National Storytelling Festival
- Gay Ducey: Teaches storytelling at University of California, Berkeley; a freelance storyteller
- Pleasant de Spain: "Seattle's Resident Storyteller"
- David Holt: Best known for appearances on the Nashville Network and host of the PBS series *Folkways*
- Bill Mooney: Starred for many years as Paul Martin on the ABC series *All My Children*
- Margaret Read MacDonald: Children's librarian and storyteller
- Rafe Martin: Award-winning author and storyteller
- J. J. Reneaux: Musician, storyteller, and writer
- Doug Lipman: Storyteller, teacher, and scholar
- Elizabeth Ellis: Professional storyteller from the Appalachian Mountains of Tennessee
- Doc McConnell: Has appeared at the National Storytelling Festival
- Gayle Ross: From the Cherokee Nation; has recorded audiotapes of Cherokee stories
- Laura Simms: Was on the board of directors for the National Storytelling Association
- Diane Ferlatte: Won awards from Parent's Choice and ALA for her audiotapes
- Bethy Horner: Former children's librarian and creative drama instructor
- Steve Sanfield: Award-winning author, poet, and storyteller
- Jon Spelman: Solo theater performer, narrative artist, monologist, and storyteller
- Joseph Bruchac: Storyteller and writer of Abenaki Indian and European ancestry
- Jim May: Storyteller who won a Chicago Emmy Award for *A Bell for Shorty*
- Jackie Torrance: Has won numerous awards and appeared at many festivals

- Barbara McBride-Smith: Full-time school librarian and traveling storyteller
- Robin Moore: Writer; has been a storyteller since 1981
- Jay O'Callahan: Has performed worldwide; created and performed stories for fifteen years
- Chuck Larkin: Has been a featured storyteller at over forty festivals
- Michael Parent: Tells stories reflecting growing up in a bilingual French Canadian family
- Donald Davis: Became a professional storyteller after growing up in a family with storytelling traditions
- Milbre Burch: Has produced tapes and published stories performed throughout the United States
- Peninnah Schram: Has been telling stories professionally since 1970
- Connie Regan Blake and Barbara Freeman: The Folktellers; recipients of the ALA Notable Recording Award, 1986
- Heather Forest: Has a unique minstrel style of storytelling
- Ed Stivender: Known for renditions of fairy tales with a comic twist
- Susan Klein: Has been featured at over thirty storytelling festivals
- Bobby Norfolk: Accomplished writer and director; blends new stories with old favorites
- Gwenda Ledbetter: Has been featured at the National Storytelling Festival

Articles about storytelling and a long list of pithy and charming quotes from famous people about storytelling and storytellers are posted at http://www.storyteller.net/tellers/p_christensen. Peruse the following sampling:

- All human beings have an innate need to hear and tell stories and to have a story to live by. . . . Religion, whatever else it has done, has provided one of the main ways of meeting this abiding mood. —Harvey Cox, *The Seduction of the Spirit*
- Story is far older than the art of science and psychology and will always be the elder in the equation no matter how much time passes. —Clarissa Pinkola Estes
- I am a storyteller. The type that went from place to place, gathered people in the square and transported them, inspired them, woke them up, shook their insides around so that they could resettle in a new pattern, a new way of being. It is a tradition that believes that the story speaks to the soul, not the ego . . . to the heart, not the head. In today's world, we yearn so to *understand*, to conquer with our mind, but it is not in the mind that a mythic story dwells. —Donna Jacobs Sife

Other quotes from Ted Talks segments featuring writers and storytellers appear at the site storytelling–quotes:tumblr.com:

- We create stories to define our existence. If we do not create stories, we probably go mad. I tell a story, and therefore I exist.—Shekhar Kapur
- Stories matter. Many stories matter. Stories have been used to dispossess and to malign, but stories can also be used to empower and to humanize. Stories can break the dignity of a people, but stories can also repair that broken dignity.—Chimamanda Noozi Adichie
- What is truer than truth? Answer: the story.—Isabel Allende, referencing a Jewish adage

NOTES

1. Chinua Achebe, in *Jump Up and Say! A Collection of Black Storytelling*, edited by Linda Goss and Clay Goss (New York: Simon and Schuster, 1995), p. 56.

2. Wendy Leonard, "Native American Tribes Bury Remains 150 Years after Massacre," *Deseret News*, May 25, 2013, updated June 3, 2013.

3. Mrs. Janie Hunter, "They Want Me to Talk about the Past," *Ain't You Got a Right to the Tree of Life? The People of Johns Island, South Carolina: Their Faces, Their Words and Their Songs*, recorded by Guy and Candie Carawan (New York: Simon and Schuster, 1966), p. 72.

4. Anne Pellowski, *The World of Storytelling* (Bronx, NY: H. W. Wilson, 1990), p. 18.

5. Student paper on Garrison Keillor from a storytelling course taught by Binnie Tate Wilkin at the University of California, Berkeley, School of Library Science, 1987.

6. Ron Jones, "North Carolina Stories and Storytellers," *Tar Heel Junior Historian* 41:2 (Spring 2002), p. 1.

7. Nancy Schimmel. *Just Enough to Make a Story* (Berkeley, CA: Sister's Choice Press, 1982), p. 2.

8. David Holt and Bill Mooney, *Ready-to-Tell Tales: Sure-Fire Stories from America's Favorite Storytellers* (Atlanta, GA: August House, 2005). Storytellers listed as they appear in the book.

FIVE

Choosing Stories to Tell

The genre and processof storytelling, the tradition of orality, is one characterized by conjuring up images, by stylistic rhythm and thematic poignancy. This, too, is the essence of poetry. — Roy Farrar[1]

In almost every library, a wide variety of story collections are available representing many themes and cultures. Browsing through collections and choosing stories that *have appeal* and seem good for telling are important first steps. Those stories that feel comfortable are also the best choices for teaching purposes. Fables and folktales generally are presented in simple progressions, making it easier to learn some of the shorter, simpler ones. After the first attempt at telling before an audience, selections can be longer. The experience of success will add confidence when trying to digest longer, more complex choices. For some, memorization is a special skill, and choices of literary tales demanding use of an author's own words pose no problems.

Story selections should be those that seem to demand sharing and those to which *natural* creative energies can be committed. To command the attention of an audience, telling stories with conviction is imperative. Reading some passages aloud helps the inexperienced recognize that some stories don't seem right for telling. Making choices involves checking a story for satisfactory beginnings, progressions, and endings. As a storyteller learns and advances, more elements assisting with choices become apparent. Using familiar titles as examples, some important factors for choice are reviewed in this chapter.

In part, the *rhythm* of some stories can be jarring. Those with rhythm that can easily be amplified in the telling feel good on the tongue when read aloud. The search is for those stories containing pleasing sounds, rhymes, and rhythms. All audiences seem to respond to alliterative language. In "Jack and the Beanstalk," each venture to the top of the giant stalk has the ogre saying, "Fee, fie, foe, fum, I smell the blood of an Englishman." In "Hansel and Gretel" as the children taste the ginger-bread house, the witch says, "Nibble, nibble, little mouse, who is nibbling at my house?" Some versions of "Cinderella" have passages in verse said by the fairy godmother.

Plots should be simple and well developed. The classic "Cinderella" tale that has been told in many versions and expanded into film is based on a fairly simple plot. A beautiful girl hated by her stepmother and stepsisters is treated like a charwoman and servant. In spite of hardships, she maintains humor and joy, having been blessed as a child by her fairy godmother. When the prince's ball is held, the servant girl is ignored, while the stepmother and stepsisters go to the ball. On this occasion, Cinderella is visited by her fairy godmother, who provides the magic of elegant dress, including shoes of spun glass. Transported to the ball, looking so gorgeous that the stepsisters and -mother don't recognize her, she dances with the prince. The prince falls in love with Cinderella, but she disappears at midnight as ordered by the fairy godmother, leaving one glass slipper. All the women in the kingdom try to fit their feet into the glass slipper, which the prince uses in search for the woman of his dreams. Only Cinderella's foot will fit the slipper, and when discovered, the prince proposes marriage, and they live happily ever after. The plot flows in simple progressions. Characters are stereotypically flat, but the evil actions of the stepmother and stepsisters invite sympathy for Cinde-rella and promotes anger at the other women. (It should be reiterated that these stories in their modern dress are far from duplicates of the original tales. Because they were not originally written for children, some original incidents and endings were brutal. Many collections retain endings of the Cinderella story with the stepsisters cutting off their toes and heels in hopes of fitting their feet into the glass slipper. One version ends with birds pecking out the stepsisters' eyes as punishment.)

Sometimes, one element of a plot will be attractive, but overall the story doesn't seem exciting. Perhaps, this is the time to look for other versions or simply discard the story. It is difficult to reshape a badly written story.

Scenes of the story should build on each other much like a cumulative narrative in which additions are made to progressive sequences. Unlike the cumulative style in Cinderella and other representative classics, the sequences are not repeated, nor are they reminders of previous scenes but are like building blocks elucidating and following the action of the plot. In "Hansel and Gretel," another folklore classic, the wicked step-mother is again present, trying to rid herself of her husband's two chil-dren because there are too many mouths to feed. In the first scenes, the children hear the parents' discussions about arranging their fate. The scene shifts when they are lost in the woods but escape and return home. Without description, it is obvious that the woods are dense when the brother foils the stepmother's plot by placing shiny flints along the way for tracking the route back home. In the next scene the children are taken back to the woods using bread to mark their way home, but alas, the bread is eaten by birds, and the scene progresses to the two children alone in the woods. The gingerbread house is found, and the evil witch entices the children into the house with plans to eat them. The rest of the scenes involve outwitting the witch. Well-written scenes are especially important to the storyteller because learning stories results from mental pictures formed by the writing.

Although personalities in popular folklore are not the rounded-out characters of good novels, the *characterizations* should be consistent and portrayed believingly from beginning to end. Unless something in the plot causes a change, a story beginning with the character of an *evil* witch should consistently present the same witch. It would be shocking if for no reason the witch suddenly became benevolent. Such structural anomalies can occur when stories have been adapted or translated from original versions. All characters should be believable in the context of the story. Cinderella's positive and joyful demeanor would not be believable without blessings given by the fairy godmother, making that demeanor believable in the context of the story. In the droll tale "Jack and the Beanstalk," Jack is characterized with lesser intelligence. After trading a cow for beans, he remains naïve throughout. Good fortune is bestowed upon him from outside forces, not as the result of educated choices. Characters should also have some appeal to the teller and hopefully the audience. The teller and listeners sympathize with Jack, in spite of his choices, as forces bigger than he are overcome.

Colorful and witty language adds to a story's usefulness for telling. In reference to a cumulative tale classic, "The Old Lady Who Swallowed a Fly" includes witty inserts to each change in sequence, which adds to the charm. When the old lady swallows the bird, the question is asked, "Isn't that absurd, she swallowed a bird?" and when she swallows the goat, "She just opened up her throat and swallowed the goat." Although this is a poetic story to be memorized, the wit and economy of language is readily apparent.

Detailed *descriptive passages* are unusual in folktales. Although adults may appreciate flowery descriptors, a storyteller must prepare for mixed audiences. Children, not having the same experience with language as an adult, may become bored with long passages with no action. They can become lost in the use of symbolic language readily understood by adults. Storytellers must remember that children do not have the benefit of historical experience. They simply have not been around long enough to understand such references as the "modern Camelot," referring to the Kennedy administration. However, too much economy of language can detract from the story's projection of imagery. "A large field of corn" engenders an entirely different image than "miles of corn planted so close the rows provided shade from the sun."

Humor is an important element to consider in searching for stories. A complete story program needs some comic relief. The level and appropriateness of merriment is of concern. Subtle innuendos may be elusive to an audience, and stories that denigrate certain classes or groups of people should be carefully avoided. Jack of the beanstalk story is the typical numbskull of a droll, but his character is *generic*. Although poor, his attributes are not assigned to a whole group. Nothing indicates that Jack is dumb *because* he is poor, and in the end he becomes rich. If a story is supposed to be humorous, it should engender smiles at each review. When a rereading falls flat, maybe that story should be discarded for one more humorous.

Children respond more readily to silly stories than do adult audiences. A story like "The Three Sillies," in which a man who never learned how to put on his pants spends each morning trying to jump into them, works well with the elementary school crowd but may bring groans from older groups. The humor of trickster tales starring Anansi and Br'er Rabbit seems to charm all audiences.

Consideration should be given to a story's *dramatic appeal*, which does not refer to acting it out but instead indicates the provision of material requiring dramatic nuances of voice. Although simplistic, "Jack and the Beanstalk" provides considerable drama in the sale of the cow, Jack's confrontation with his mother, his tossing the beans, and the growth of the stalk. Encounters with the ogre's wife and the final confrontation with the ogre are ripe for dramatic voice usage. In contrast, "Cinderella" starts with dramatic descriptions, eliciting sympathy from the audience, but spritely drama occurs when the fairy godmother reappears. After this sequence, action and suspense gain strength, ending with frantic efforts to claim ownership of the glass slipper. Depending upon the version encountered, in "Hansel and Gretel" drama is palpable throughout. At the beginning, two children become aware of plans to banish them to the woods. Survival becomes the focus until the dramatic discovery of the gingerbread house, continuing until the witch is outwitted and the children escape.

Necessary to almost any plot, with the exception of "mood pieces" designed to lull a child to sleep, *action* provides much of the pacing to be applied through the voice of the storyteller. When Jack climbs and climbs and climbs the beanstalk, the action is deliberate and anticipatory. When running from the ogre, the movement is based in fear and later continues on a straight path to the climax. The fairy godmother's actions, changing Cinderella's dress and sending her to the ball, infers something else is about to happen. Winding down, after the glass shoe is fitted, the action quiets to a satisfactory ending.

The *mood* of a story is a factor to be considered in making selections. "Jack and the Beanstalk" presents the humorous mood of a droll. The background of humor is set early when Jack succumbs to treachery, exchanging a cow for beans. The mood then follows the action after the beanstalk grows and adventures begin. In "Hansel and Gretel," extreme poverty and threat of banishing children to the woods set a somber mood. The somber atmosphere continues through the children's capture by the witch. At this point there is a mood of fearful expectancy and hope for the children's escape. Similarly in "Cinderella," early passages create a mood of distress. Only Cinderella's demeanor and the return of the fairy godmother lighten the mood.

Another measure of a good selection is finding *nothing extraneous to the story*. Some writers and storytellers are prone toward attaching elements to the story for purposes of introducing a message. Such added phrases or passages can be disconcerting to listeners. Any placement of new characters or scenes in a story should have a reason to which readers and audiences can relate. In efforts to adapt a story to suit certain expectations, extraneous items unfaithful to the source are sometimes added. The result is the same as finding a 1950s car in a story, film, or video set in the 1920s.

Social protests bring objections to some stories and story types. During the height of the women's liberation movement, fairy tales and the "princess" image were called into question. Attempts were made to rewrite stories from a feminist point of view. However, twentieth-century attitudes sometimes did not work well in a seventeenth-century tale reflecting seventeenth-century norms. There are good stories to be used in support of social issues, but storytellers must respond carefully to their own "missions" or outside demands for change. With the help of the library, the Internet, and listening to others, very good stories on almost all subjects can be found.

Themes of some narratives are more clearly defined than in others, and multiple themes can be derived from one story. In many ways, theme equates to motif—those methods and meanings central to the story. The "princess" theme of "Cinderella" in the social context of the times could have referenced the persecuted being saved and finding fortune. The "Hansel and Gretel" motif of the poor in distress is much the same and is repeated in "Jack and the Beanstalk," except that fortune comes to a *poor boy without much intellect*. With searching and speculation, other subthemes may be found. The best stories for telling establish a central theme and move it throughout the story.

Personal Note: When I first started telling stories. I found myself reading and reading and reading. This process proved both valuable and overwhelming. I began to build a file of probably two hundred stories with notes. Then I tried sorting them to be made available when certain types of subject matter were requested. The resulting value of this exercise was developing a sense of the story and finding proof of the many cultural overlaps of theme or motif. Those cultures whose stories were always close to nature and gave reverence to animal life as well as the human existence became evident. Soon, it was realized that placing and retaining all these stories in memory would be problematic. Eventually a file was added in front of the larger file titled "Stories to Learn." These would be my basic repertoire. Over the years, that group of stories became smaller as I returned so often to favorites. It became a challenge to occasionally add others. Like comedians and other artists, I found myself telling many of the same stories over and over again. With this repetition of telling, I began to *own* stories that became a real part of my life and psyche. I could retrieve them when necessary but not always in the same format.

When choosing stories that include cultural or ethnic information and references, it is especially important to check for accuracy and authenticity. Several good stories structurally have met with criticism because of inaccurate cultural references and portrayals. Examples are *The Five Chinese Brothers* and *Tikki Tikki Tembo*. Complaints are made about the pictures portraying faces that all seem the same and of men wearing cues in a story created long after this hairstyle was worn. Concerning *Tikki Tikki Tembo*, several persons of Chinese heritage argue that such names were never found in their culture. Others say the story is folklore, not a history of names. One claim has been made that *Tikki Tikki Tembo* is an authentic *Japanese* story, appropriated to another culture. These complaints come from people within the culture represented. Although counterarguments exist, it seems wise to follow the lead of those within the culture rather than cause embarrassment. There are enough stories available to allow storytellers the choice of ignoring those that make them or perspective audiences uncomfortable. The controversies about these stories are available in library literature and on the Internet. Lists of stories from a variety of cultures may be obtained from local libraries or the American Library Association's Office of Literacy and Outreach Services (OLOS).

In the early stages of becoming a storyteller, choosing stories with difficult or many names to remember should probably be avoided to make the task of learning easier. Names must always be memorized, although the rest of a story allows some flexibility.

It is possible to tell modern stories, stories from picture books, biographical narratives, excerpts from novels, and original stories, although professional storytellers should carefully analyze copyright laws. Some choices will come from having heard a successful telling. It will prove expedient to look for selections allowing call and response or audience involvement. These will be handy tools when audiences are hard to quiet or disruptions are experienced. Concerned about rising cultures of violence, some storytellers are avoiding folktales containing excessive violent actions or changing them for the telling. Storytellers must use their own discretion in making such decisions.

There is nothing wrong with telling personal stories, being careful not to use names and places without permission. The danger is that most personal stories are remembered as anecdotes, not fully formed narratives, and as a result, responses can be a disappointment. Building a repertoire is an important task. Those stories that bring joy to the storyteller and audience will be told repeatedly. One storyteller has suggested that one should commit to learning a new story every year and that it might help to set a particular date or time for that endeavor. Nancy Schimmel advises:

> While it's a good idea to tell only stories you like it is possible to find a kind of story you like and feel safe with, and not try other kinds—to tell only funny stories, or fairy tales, or whatever your preference is. Not that you should feel bad about neglecting a kind you don't like after you've given it a fair try. . . . But you never know—a little experimenting, even under duress, may open up to you a whole body of stories you never thought you could tell.[2]

NOTE

1. Roy Farrar (quote) in *Jump Up and Say, A Collection of Black Storytelling* by Linda Goss and Clay Goss (New York: Simon and Schuster, 1995), p. 23.
2. Nancy Schimmel, *Just Enough to Make a Story: A Sourcebook for Storytelling*, 2nd edition (Berkeley, CA: Sister's Choice Press, 1978, 1982), p. 4.

SIX

Reading, Adaptation, and Learning

It is something like stumbling upon a mountain stream. You can free yourself in the play of light and shade along the surface. You can taste the clear, cold water. Eventually you can follow the stream to where it joins up with many others, a living flowing system that we call the oral tradition—Joseph Daniel Sobol[1]

Storytelling requires learning the sequences and actions of a story, not the memorization of words. In the past, sectors of storytellers demanded word-for-word recitation of the entire story as written by the author. Today, most experts believe that because the story form evolved from simple folk telling tales around a fire, each storyteller should be allowed to present stories in their own manner and in their *own* words.

The arguments about committing stories to memory are similar to those in education. For years there have been arguments about the amount of information a student retains after participating in "rote" learning and memorization of facts and figures. Teachers who help students to place facts and figures in the context of larger pictures claim retention of that knowledge is more permanent. For the storyteller, learning a story for effective communication with audiences is the goal. Either choice made by the teller, to memorize or to form mental sequences and patterns, requires asking some of the following questions: What was the source of the story? What was its purpose? Will it be effective when told rather than read? If well prepared and done effectively, there is nothing wrong with reading aloud. Preparing a reading requires sufficient time, although the tedium is less. The process of learning may be easier for some but a chore for others. As emphasized in the previous chapter, it is especially important to choose stories to which a commitment can be made to learn. Effective methods of learning and presenting a story have been suggested by many. Following is a capsulation of directives and other suggestions.

Consider that the minds of the audience are canvases upon which you wish to paint the pictures from your story. Learning will mean outlining those pictures in your own mind.

Always review the whole story so that your memory of events will remain balanced. This way, you are less likely to forget a segment that does not stand out in your mind.

Allow a time for learning, with a relaxed space to spend with the story. When you have chosen the story you desire to tell, read it several times, preferably out loud. Read for a sense of the story, and notice the details. Sometimes it helps to read the story aloud on tape and listen to the tape repeatedly. The sensory process of hearing may start to implant sequences in the mind and will assist in the visualization process necessary later. Students have complained about taping because they find the recording of their voices disconcerting. First-time tellers are surprised at the way they sound. Voices on tape sound different from the way tellers hear themselves daily. The advantage of *reading out loud* is that the sounds and rhythms of the story can be tried out on the tongue. While reading or listening to a tape, CD, or DVD, some considerations are: What are the feelings and emotions experienced? What are the tastes and sounds in the story? Are there scenes that especially stand out, and are there enough such scenes to keep an audience captivated? Consider what senses are stimulated from your reading of the tale. For example, when telling "Stone Soup," imagining the smell as people bring more and more items to add to the stew takes the story to another dimension. Once this is done, the story begins to become alive in the teller and will be easier to remember.

Research the story's background, and live with the narrative until its characters become familiar associates. Learning the story as a whole and not in fragments may be very important for maintaining the unity of the tale. Study and recognize the style, realizing all tellers add something of their own style to all presentations.

Outline the story on paper, paying attention to the sequence of action, and visualize the characters taking these actions. Paint the details into your visual memory. The teller's visual memory will be translated as the story is told, while listeners will form their own visions.

Review the sequence of the story, and slowly add the details of place and setting.

Determine if there are short phrases, lines, songs, or chants that should be memorized word for word. Especially for beginners, if the choice is made for including such passages, they should be short and uncomplicated.

Practice telling the story out loud. Tell it to yourself in the mirror, to your cat, to your dog, to your partner or spouse, and to an imaginary audience. After learning the story thoroughly, it will become clear that the better a story is known, the fewer times it will be told the same. In today's world, with the constant bombardment of images imposed by others, useless trivia is absorbed and made part of our psyches. Storytelling and listening to stories allows the chance to create images for ourselves.

Write the story outline a second time. Read it several times, reviewing mental pictures of each sequence, and then try the first telling before an imaginary audience. Without worry about missed passages, completing the story is important. Rewrite the outline a third and final time, *trying not to use notes*. Areas needing the most concentration will become apparent.

Tell the story again, especially when it seems that all is right. By this time, a feeling of security should be developed. The learning session is over, but the story should be practiced several times before a program. Two practice outlines of stories found in chapter 10 follow.

THE BREMEN TOWN MUSICIANS: AN OUTLINE FOR LEARNING

- Donkey: Too old to carry burdens anymore. Fears owner will get rid of him.
- Runs away, hoping to become the Bremen town musician.
- On the way, he meets Dog.
- Dog: Too old to hunt anymore. Fears his owner will get rid of him.
- Donkey asks Dog to join him. Maybe they can make music together.
- The two travel together.
- On the way they meet Cat.
- Cat: Too old to kill mice anymore. Fears owner will replace him.
- Donkey asks him to come along and join him and Dog in making music.
- The three travel together.
- On the way they meet Rooster.
- Rooster: Crows with all his might because he fears his sound is weak and he might be cooked for dinner.
- Donkey asks him to come along, thinking that together Donkey, with Dog, with Cat, and with Rooster cannot be refused as Bremen's town musicians.
- Night falls, and the four animals sleep, Donkey and Dog on the ground, Cat and Rooster in the tree.
- They see the lights of a house in the distance and decide to go there.
- At the house, Donkey looks in the window and sees thieves counting their loot on the table.
- Donkey devises a plan.

- Donkey stands at the window, Dog stands on Donkey, Cat stands on Dog, and Rooster stands on Cat.
- On the signal, they all sing (Donkey brays, Dog barks, Cat meows, and Rooster crows). The song (noise) frightens the robbers, who run from the house.
- The four animals stay.
- Later, the robbers reconsider and return to the house, thinking it may have been foolish to leave all their loot.
- One robber is sent in to investigate.
- In the dark, he is bitten by Dog, kicked by Donkey, scratched by Cat, and hears Rooster crow loudly.
- Robber runs and returns to his friends and explains that they can't return to that house because it is haunted.
- Donkey, Dog, Cat, and Rooster stay in the house and live happily ever after.

Tell your version to someone, and have fun with it!

When first starting, find a forgiving audience of whom you are not frightened. School classes offer this opportunity. Audiences usually respond to your enthusiasm. A local storytelling group or guild is another place to tell and find helpful critiques. Over the days, weeks, and years, the telling gets better and better.

The story "Nomi and the Magic Fish" is a Cinderella motif from an entirely different culture than the Grimm version. Small elements place the story in a different culture.

NOMI AND THE MAGIC FISH: AN OUTLINE FOR LEARNING

- Nomi, the main character, is lovely, tall, slender, and brown.
- Her mother died when she was young, and her father remarried.
- Stepmother has a daughter not as attractive as Nomi. The stepsister, named Nomsa, is self-centered and mean.
- Stepmother hates Nomi and assigns her all the hard work. She feeds Nomi and her dog scraps of food. Nomi and Dog grow thin.
- Daily, Nomi is sent to the veld to tend cattle.
- Stepmother instructs, "Take the cows to the veld, and don't come for lunch; there is no food."
- One day in the veld, Nomi takes the cattle to the pool for water. Tired and hungry, she sits down and begins to cry.
- A fish in the pool speaks to Nomi. She has seen the fish there before.
- Fish asks, "Why are you crying?"
- Nomi answers, "I'm tired and hungry. My stepmother hates me. Look how thin I am getting."

- Fish says, "You must not tell anyone, but I can bring food for you and your dog."
- Every day, Nomi and Dog receive food from Fish. Both regain their weight.
- Stepmother soon notices the change.
- Stepmother asks, " Where are you getting food?" Nomi doesn't answer, will not reveal the secret.
- Stepmother beats her more with a stick with no result. Then she beats Dog, who tells the secret.
- Dog says, "There is a fish in the pond in the veld who gives us food."
- Nomi runs to warn Fish.
- Fish says, "The woman will surely kill me, but you must remember to save my bones and throw them in the chief's garden."
- Next morning, Stepmother pretends to be sick. She tells her husband, "I need some fish. I'm sure if I had fish, I would feel better. There is one down in the veld in a pond. Catch it, and cook it for me."
- Stepfather does as asked. Kills and cooks Fish.
- After Fish is eaten, Nomi, cleans up everything, saving Fish's bones.
- Nomi throws bones in the garden of the chief.
- Chief is out to walk, discovers the bones, calls his attendant. The attendant can't pick them up. They simply slip between his fingers.
- Chief calls many to try picking up those bones. Offers reward of wealth to anyone who can pick up the bones.
- All in the village try.
- Chief asks, "Is that everyone? Is there no one else who might be able to move those bones?"
- Villagers remember that Nomi has not been there to try.
- Chief sends for Nomi. She easily picks up the bones.
- She is rewarded and betrothed to the prince.

As the scenes are imagined and painted in the mind, the teller will feel emotions and learn to translate those emotions with the voice. This story provides many opportunities for nuances of the voice—the angry stepmother, Nomi feeling sad and hungry, and the violent scene when Nomi and Dog are hit.

At first, the hardest translations to be made may be when characters are animals, as in the "Bremen Town Musicians" story. The animals now are anthropomorphic *persons*, with animal features and actions. Thinking of each animal as having a certain personality or emotion will aid in the learning. Seek that "I've got it!" moment when the goal—*ownership of the story*—is reached. Most important is the *desire to learn and share*.

ADAPTATION

For many reasons, stories are continually adapted. Moving from place to place and from culture to culture, passages are added and deleted. A storyteller may find the necessity to adapt a tale, the most common reason being time allotment. In these cases a story may be shortened, but care must be taken to retain the sense of the story. Stories with repeat sequences can be shortened simply by saying, "And on the third trip, the result was exactly the same as the first two," without all the details and description, and, "But this time, she said the name . . ." There might be an occasion when the teller would like the story to last a little longer. This can be done by adding descriptive passages because folktales commonly have few descriptions. In either of these cases, the revamping of the story should be done very carefully. If descriptions are added, they *must* be appropriate for the time and place of the story.

The age or nature of an audience may be reason for adapting a story. Stories with adult content in some cases can be simplified for a younger audience. As discussed earlier, some storytellers elect to remove or soften scenes of violence.

Personal Note: Years ago, I began examining my presentation of witches after meeting women who designated themselves as witches as a cultural choice. Portraying all witches as old hags became problematic. In some cases I found it very easy to say, "A woman with strange and special powers" or "A mythical goddess."

Some stories can be adapted for a special celebration by simply having the events happen on that day. The old story of "The Pancake" could be any food that you make roll or run away or that you wish to represent, possibly *hamburgers* or *hot dogs*.

NOTES

1. Joseph Daniel Sobol (quote) in *Southern Jack Tales* by Donald Davis (Little Rock, AR: August House, 1992), p. 11.

SEVEN

Developing Personal Style

There are no great studied gestures here, no tricks of changing voices to suit each character of the story, no costumes nor gimmicks to substantiate the tale. Above all, there is no condescension, either to the story or to the children, no pseudo-ecstatic tone of voice that some adults assume when speaking to children, no asking of questions before and after, no insistence on explanations of the meanings of words, no rewards for listening—except the story itself.—Ruth Sawyer[1]

Terminology commonly applied to successful storytelling is "bringing the story alive," which basically means the teller establishes an emotional connection with audience. Fleshing out characters into living beings requires *prior* suspension of disbelief by the storyteller. Only then can the audience be presented the same challenge. Animals, ghosts, gods, and heroes are seen as real in the mind of the purveyor, who transports listeners on the temporary journey to belief. To accomplish this, it bears repeating, tellers must choose stories that they enjoy or with which they have some emotional connection. Fear, surprise, hurt, and more emotions transfer to the listener when characters are alive in the mind of the storyteller. Through natural nuances of voice and facial expression, emotions become evident without any phony actions by the teller.

The tone of stories varies with intention to challenge, to capture the imagination, and to speak of those things human in each person. Pacing, rhythm, loudness, speed, silence, and active pauses gradually become a seasoned storyteller's tools for effective communication. Feeling entirely comfortable with the story sharing and having confidence will allow the eventual inclusion of audience participation as a feature of presentation. Call and response is one effective tool for engaging attention. Other methods of commanding a group include simple but interesting introductions. Depending upon the setting, an audience can be engaged with a beginning chant or "Once upon a time" or "Once a long time ago." One storyteller uses "Guess what. I had a dream last night." Introductory phrases bring the audience to the story, but long explanations before the story can be disconcerting and distract the audience's thoughts in unknown ways.

Personal Note: "Hello, everyone. I am Bibi Binnie, a storyteller" and "Jambo! Jambo! Jambo means 'hello,'" are greetings I have used. If rumblings are heard in the Personal Note – "Hello everyone, I am Bibi Binnie, a storyteller" and "Jambo! Jambo!, Jambo means hello, hello," are greetings I have used. If rumblings are heard in the audience, I've said, "Let me hear you audience: 'Jambo! Jambo! Jambo means "hello."'" Immediately I move into the story. It has been my practice never to give the title of the story but to begin, "Once there were three boys" or "Once, in a small Haitian village many years ago" or the introductions previously mentioned begins the story. At the end I say, "That story was called . . ." Some stories have first lines that serve as outstanding invitations. "Once there were four boys who lived in a cave. They had no mother or father" is an example. There is no need for introductions. Endings are easier, and the classic one, "Snip, snap, snout, this tale's told out" still works. I like using the African ending "If it be sweet, take some and send some back to me." Sad endings I let speak for themselves, taking a few steps back, signaling "the end." When telling real stories, in my case mostly biographical stories, it seems easier and most effective to use a first-person narrative, beginning, "I am Sojourner Truth. My birth name was Isabella." At this time, the telling becomes a one-person performance. These stories are usually designed for educational programs or celebrations of special events. The mission is to arouse interest in a personality and hopefully encourage further exploration. Audiences have accepted these offerings as an extension of storytelling.

Style represents a combination of personality, the sincere wish to communicate, and artistic development. For some story performers, it means the addition of gimmicks, artifacts, music, and games. The factor of central importance for a storyteller is use of the voice. Characteristics of reading aloud, reciting, and acting are present, but the process is not exactly the same. The storyteller looks into the eyes of the audience, literally or symbolically, and together they compose the tale. Artistic storytellers see and recreate a series of mental images while responding every moment to audience reaction and changing the telling accordingly. The assumption is that each listener will compose their own story from the mental images they form. Each person's visions will be entirely different from others listening to the same story but hearing with a different viewpoint or from a different emotional place. When reading storytelling literature and listening to a variety of storytelling critics, numerous opinions about style will be found. There is no stylistic *right* or *wrong*, instead, the method that accomplishes effective communication of the story is *right*.

Naturally, some people have quiet voices; others project loudly. Many feel comfortable "hamming it up," while others prefer straightforward sharing. The following are clues to avoiding pitfalls.

VOICE SHADING

The voice is all that is needed to provide the proper shading for a story. Practice shading with a story, such as "The Teeny Tiny Woman." The repetition of the words *teeny tiny* could be very boring if said exactly the same on each repeat. Modulating the voice slightly during changes will help keep the audience interested and attentive. Using a "small" voice throughout can be equally problematic, but using the small voice only when the woman speaks breaks the monotony. At the end of the story, each time the ghostly voice returns seeking the bone, the voice can be a little larger and louder, ending with the final shout, "Take it!"

Ruth Sawyer, in her book *The Way of the Storyteller*, emphasizes use of the voice. She feels that a storyteller's instrument, much like a singer, is his or her voice. Serious storytellers aiming at making a living with the art might investigate some of her techniques for strengthening and caring for the voice. The following quote speaks volumes:

> Something happened to my voice that night. I remembered all things John Denis Meehan had taught me about reality of tone; that no honest, convincing sound came out of a human being short of the diaphragm and abdominal muscles. For the first time that night I brought my stories up from below my belt-line. Every word was spoken with physical vigor and a faith that could almost move mountains.[2]

PACING AND TIMING

It must be remembered that folk stories do not concentrate on the characters but on the plot. Pacing of that plot to entice listeners requires focus. Unusual twists in the story demand distinct changes in pace, voice, and mood. Different pacing for a story may need experimentation. A story told at the same pace throughout will lack interest. Consider the effectiveness of the line "He ran lickety-split down the road" being delivered at a slow deliberate pace. The speed, slowness, or necessity for pauses should *feel real*.

CREATING VOICES FOR CHARACTERS

The use of simulated voices may be popular and seem like fun, but the practice gives a storyteller one more thing to remember. Each time a character appears, the storyteller must remember the voice selected. Use of posture or facial expressions to exhibit different characters should be easier than trying to use voices. Those expressions should not be forced but allowed to surface naturally. Practiced expressions will be distractingly evident. The voice should be used for pauses, to represent tension, or for dramatic emphasis. All of this will come much easier once a story is thoroughly captured in memory. The presentation will feel like a real story told to a friend or neighbor with all the appropriate drama and emphasis.

Loudness and softness are effective tools. Instead of a scruffy voice in the story of "The Three Billy Goats Gruff" when the ogre speaks, a louder voice may suffice. As noted earlier, voice inflection and modulation are important and combined with an air of authority and sincerity lead to quality performances. If a funny, too soft, or whiny voice different from the teller's own is chosen, audiences may find these portrayals humorous when the intent was serious. If imitative voices are used, they must be thoroughly prepared, just as an actor learns to portray a dialect. Observation of storytellers over many years has revealed the hazard of forgetting selected voices. Some are successful at spending the necessary time mastering voices and dialects and move into them with an ease that is charming and effective.

"Uncle Remus Tales" were originally written in an almost unreadable exaggerated dialect considered appealing. Many African Americans considered this use of language demeaning. The best users of dialects as a second voice are those people for whom that dialect is *already a second language.*

AUDIENCE AWARENESS

Individual style must be uniquely personal, although elements of style can be created or copied. Each intriguing style of storytelling probably draws on the methods of others. *Emphasis* but not basic style can change depending upon the venue. Audiences have an important role in storytelling. Consideration is always given to what the audience seems to desire. Preparation for a story presentation questions what strategies are necessary to translate the storyteller's feelings to the audience. What are the adjustments needed to transmit those emotions experienced by the performer and to capture listeners in the web of lore?

There is, in the opinion of many, a difference between storytelling and performing a story. Because some people are naturally dramatic, drama shows in their faces and body movements without effort. But, the addition of movement, dance, song, and games to a story program becomes a performance. Engaging large audiences or a full auditorium usually requires some drama. In such cases, it is impossible to maintain eye contact as with a smaller audience. The storyteller must call upon abilities to *project* and to *sense* how the audience is responding. Sometimes, focusing occasionally on a few faces visible in the front rows is helpful.

Adult audiences may attend programs with several motivations—to be empowered, to enjoy a metaphor, to be reminded of childhood, to reinforce beliefs, or all of above. Although telling the story requires concentration, audience awareness will add to overall effectiveness. When reaction is seen upon faces or heard in audible gasps, help is given to the artist. Considering the necessity to actively involve the audience will be determined by these clues.

Young audiences may be called upon to participate in phrases that are repeated over and over throughout the story, such as "Trip-trap, trip-trap, trip-trap" in "Three Billy Goats Gruff." Such phrases are available in many stories. Also asking "Can you guess what happened?" can restore attention. If the storyteller completely loses an audience, the story should be ended quickly and a participation story or poem inserted.

"Kric Krac," or "Crick Crack," is a style common to the Caribbean. The audience is called upon to participate throughout. This style is successful with audiences after repeat encounters but may not work as well otherwise. As a simulation, the following can be used: "When I say 'crick crack,' you say 'crick crack.' When I say 'crick,' you say 'crack.' When I say 'crick,' if you want a story, say 'crack.'" This proves to be fun when inserted at odd times during the story program.

Storytellers having a style that separates them or allows them to withdraw from the audience may have little success. Even when the performing storyteller temporarily withdraws into the character, the style must allow for reconnection to occur. Years ago, however, a storyteller was observed doing paper folding while storytelling. She managed to withdraw while folding and return to audience with successful timing.

It is the habit of some tellers to *move* constantly before their audience. Repercussions can occur with this method when sophisticated audio equipment is unavailable. Many places, such as schools, have limited equipment, and telling to large audiences requires being placed before a stationary microphone. Requests can be made for a battery pack or an attachable mike. While developing style, a storyteller must give consideration to such possible limitations and be prepared to adjust accordingly. No matter what the style, it is most important to know the stories well, so that restlessness and interruptions can be handled The best performers will be prepared with substitute stories, preferably requiring active involvement. *Joining In: An Anthology of Audience Participation Stories and How to Tell Them* by Teresa Miller, Anne Pellowski, and Norma J. Livo contains stories that involve audience participation.

Personal Note: On assignment to do storytelling at a huge Los Angeles City street festival, I assumed the storytelling venue would be separate from the large, milling crowds. As it turned out, I was assigned to the main large platform, with hundreds of people around everywhere. Upon seeing this, I discarded the story of choice and reminded adults and children nearby of "The Old Lady Who Swallowed a Fly," which I told once, while some followed along. There was an enthusiastic response. One of downtown Los Angeles's resident drunks yelled in a slurring voice, "Tell it again, tell it again!" The crowd, the drunk, and I repeated the entire rhyming story.

ENTHUSIASM AND ANIMATION

Gestures are fine, especially if they come naturally. Other motions as part of the story are fun for children, especially the very young, but too many false gestures add an unnecessary responsibility. When a story *becomes your own*, motions and intonations will be automatic. These will change according to audience response. Practiced gestures should be used only when absolutely necessary or if a teller's natural gesturing is too distracting. Choreographed gestures often appear robotic and contrived. Being animated instead means to exude a spark of energy, almost as an electric current to the audience. Enthusiasm is much the same. It shows in the voice, facial expression, and manner of presentation.

RAMBLING

A long, rambling style, natural for some, may have the most need of correction. These storytellers seem to lack one important talent, that is, the ability to focus on the audience and recognize when they have lost them. There is also a tendency to ramble at the *end* of a story. When the story is finished, it is best to stop, not explain nor teach.

In the end, the most effective style may be the one used when talking about what happened on Saturday night or when looking out the window at an exciting development. Tuning in to that ownership, that desire to share excitement about the events, and the hope that the person listening feels some of that same stimulation in translation is the way of a storyteller. When a prepared story is presented in this manner, the telling should be most successful. Trying to build an extensive repertoire rapidly may be less than fruitful. After learning a few stories well, they can be used repeatedly. The better a story is known, the easier it will be to allow individual style to develop with ease.

Ruth Sawyer is one of the names to which almost every class and workshop referred while studying storytelling in library school and post–library school. Sawyer graduated from Columbia University in 1904, having studied folklore and storytelling. She began the first story-telling program at the New York Public Library. Spending time in Cuba teaching teachers to tell stories added to her recognition. She wrote several children's books and in 1965 received the Laura Ingalls medal for her contributions to children's literature. Her book, *The Way of the Storyteller*, continues to be recommended for her approaches to use of voice and style.

Following are personal observations of *differences in style*.

ANNE PELLOWSKI

Anne Pellowski, renown for her storytelling and books about this genre, spoke and did workshops at the American Library Association, some of which I attended. She spoke several languages and offered stories from a variety of cultures. With her facility in languages and her international experience, she was able to transport the listener into other cultures with ease. For others, this will not be quite so easy, for using other languages requires knowledge and practice. Pellowski has a tall and commanding presence that attracts audiences to her, even before the telling.

AUGUSTA BAKER

Augusta Baker was well known for telling "Uncle Bouquoi Tales." She is from the New York Public Library School of storytelling, which advocated memorized stories. However, in my observation of her, she seems to have added her own "touch" to the stories. The humor in the tales was reflected in her face as she captures the audience with her presence.

RICHARD CHASE

Richard Chase visited Los Angeles on several occasions. He wore a beret, cocked sassily on his head. While telling his famous "Jack" tales, he periodically sat on a stool or in a rocking chair. His storytelling was sometimes droll and at other times animated. It was his pacing of the story that makes him most effective.

PURA BELPRÉ

Pura Belpré, a Puerto Rican storyteller and writer whom I heard in New York City and at the American Library Association, told stories in a sparkling manner matching her personality. Her face reflected her joy in telling.

JACKIE TORRANCE

Jackie Torrance, also known for telling "Jack Tales," sometimes sat in a chair but was still quite animated in her telling. She told long tales that captivated her audiences. I heard her at a Unitarian church in Schenecta-dy, New York. Her voice was pleasing to hear, and the expressions on her face led the audience along the journey of her various "Jack" escapades.

FRANCES CLARKE SAYERS

Frances Clark Sayers and I told stories on the same stage at the Claremont Reading Conference in the early 1970s. Sayers told "Br'er Rabbit" tales. It was her sense of authority that sold audiences on her telling.

In addition to these renowned storytellers, there have been many others I've heard who exhibit or devise their own "style." One librarian-story-teller at the Los Angeles City Library devised a "story hat" that she wears when telling stories at schools and other events. On strings hung around the hat are characters from stories. Children are given a chance to peruse the characters and pick those of their choice, enough to fill the story program for that day. Obviously, she has to be very prepared.

Also, at special celebrations in Los Angeles, I met an African American gentleman, always dressed in overalls and colorful shirts, call-ing himself a "country" storyteller, while another told stories from Africa accented with drumming.

A very effective, female Chinese storyteller has a quiet-spoken but engaging way of telling. She always stands almost still, with hands clasped, but as with others, her authority in telling captures the audience.

At a storytelling workshop presented for the community and librar-ians in Los Angeles, a local minister participated. When the participants demonstrated what they learned, he told the story of Samson. In addition to authority in telling, the rhythm and cadence from years of preaching was used in the telling, revealing an effective style with which he had become comfortable.

At the Los Angeles City Library, a male librarian did a very good job of telling stories in both English and Spanish. He became so accom-plished and his face and body were so engaging that the continuity of the story was not broken for either the Spanish-speaking or English-speaking audiences.

Effective storytelling is an entrancing and beautiful art. A well-devel-oped and carefully presented story can cut across barriers and hold the interest of listeners. Stories and storytellers are remembered for a life-time. Knowing and applying the basics of storytelling strengthens indi-vidual telling and general demand.

NOTES

1. Ruth Sawyer, *The Way of the Storyteller* (New York: Viking, 1942, 1962), pp. 87–89.

2. Sawyer, *Way of the Storyteller*, pp. 87–89.

EIGHT

Stories with Dance and Movement

> Nigerian girls create a beautiful series of movements with the simple, everyday task of pounding the millet. Working the pestle in a down-and-up motion, they move in lovely counter rhythm. . . . As the human body can bring rhythm and movement to everyday tasks, so it can re-create situations by exaggerating and abstracting these very movements into mime. Think of the movement you would make to frighten somebody. Quite naturally, your body would lean forward, menacingly, the hand clenched in a fist raised in the air. You can see how stamping, shouting and waving is the most natural thing in the world. —Lee Warren[1]

The classic art of storytelling has developed in western culture as a "stand-alone," narrative process, while in Africa and in various tribal cultures of America's first nations, dance is more often than not an integral part of storytelling rituals. In general, westerners have become observers of the arts rather than participants. Across the world, "folk dance" still exists, providing a subcultural process involving average folks in plays, dance, and storytelling. Study of the arts or active participation in drama, music, and dance are no longer priorities in many American schools. Recommendation of this style of story performance is an attempt to partially address this problem. Participation in movement, no matter how limited, also challenges leaders and groups to examine and correct tendencies toward sedentary lifestyles.

In almost every culture, there seems to be some history of communal dance. In the United States, folk dance and group dances, particularly line dancing, are perpetuated in some circles. At recreation centers and special venues, line-dance groups can be found still doing the reels and other movements that trace back to Western European beginnings. In Los Angeles, when working as a cultural specialist, I found Korean, Chinese, Japanese, and East Indian dance groups ready to perform traditional dances for library-sponsored events. In African American communities' large parties and family gatherings, it is not unusual to find line dancing like the "electric slide," particularly well known by the older generation and being joined in by everyone present. In general, however, the dance of the "folk" is an uncommon finding in communities and in schools. Modern styles of disco, break dancing, and individual rhythm designs are more popular among the young.

It is the folk dances that more closely resemble my idea of presenting story with dance and movement. Many of these dances, in all cultures, were choreographed to accompany work or to simulate the work of the day and important events. The movements were simple, almost like mime set to music. The people tell stories of their everyday life as they visualize it and reproduce those visions into movements accompanied by song. After becoming familiar to and accepted by the community, the same dances became "traditional" folk dances. For example, in the story program included in chapter 9 as a sample of multicultural programming, a Japanese work dance is listed. The dance was taught to a group in which I participated by a representative from the Japanese Cultural Center in Los Angeles. The movements simulate work done building railroads in the early history of the United States. It begins with steps and swings of the arms as if pounding a hammer, breaking rocks in mountain or ground. The other movement repeated many times is a swinging side to side as if shoveling dirt. One, two, three, dig, scoop, throw, and dig, scoop, throw to the other side.

Similarly, for me the stories best used for presentation in dance are those that can provide such actions to be simulated into dance. Whenever children or audiences are asked to participate with the teller, they must be able to easily visualize the movements being mimed or danced.

Our bodies were built for movement, and our minds, if allowed, will respond to the music and visualization. Many ancient drawings and pictographs include some type of group dancing. In many cultures the dance and the music was directly tied to the myths, gods, and rituals of worship. There also is a record of recreational dance done just for the joy of it or to portray a story of the hunt, imitations of animals, and other life events. In the western world, modern-day music and dance has become entertainment and is no longer an essential part of religious rituals designed to communicate with the ancestral spirits and the gods. Some remnants of religious rites danced as well as sung can be found in a few churches but flourish mostly in places around the world where communal ties have great strength.

On the topic of East Indian music, in *Ancient and Oriental Music*, Romain Goldron discusses how essential music and dance were depictions of the power and essence of the gods. He states, "Man was by no means excluded from this concert. His whole body absorbed the exuberant sounds bestowed on him by the gods. Music affected his stomach, his heart and his head. . . . 'To his head, fount of intelligence, it devotes rhythm, the essence of life.'" [2] In a later section about Chinese music, he quotes from a treatise assigned to Confucius: "The natural expression of joy is speech. When this emotion is particularly strong, word alone cannot express it, and so speech is imperceptibly transformed into song. This inspires a feeling of ecstasy in which *bodily movement is inevitable; hand and foot gestures gradually blossom into dancing.*" [3]

Personal Note: It was during the time period when I served as children's specialist in a federally funded outreach project at the Los Angeles City Library that I first presented a story with dance. I was the children's services consultant to and program planner for nine library branches in the central region of Los Angeles. A librarian at a small library branch in the Inglewood area called me to consult about her plans for a Christmas program. Her problem was that the outreach was working a little too well. Story programs were crowded and caused children to be inattentive, especially during celebratory days. She asked me to please think of something and to appear as her guest storyteller. Thinking about the problem, I decided that maybe this situation demanded more than the traditional forms of storytelling, something that commanded attention. I learned a story called "The Christmas Rose." Having taken some courses in modern dance, I practiced translating the story into dance. On the day of the program, the small branch was packed. Before telling the story, I asked everyone to listen carefully and then to watch when I danced an interpretation of the story and see if they could recognize the story sequences and characters. It worked! The children listened quietly and loved the dancing.

It was after that occasion that more stories with dance and movement were developed. My first attempts at presenting stories with dance were not with African stories. They were stories activated into dance to see if the method, designed here, continued to have appeal and to control difficult audiences. Remember, I was not a trained dancer, although I had taken some undergraduate and community dance classes, nor did I have what would be considered a "classic" dancer's body. I simply tried to build upon the success of that first adventure with the Christmas story. Instinctively, stories that presented strong visualizations and very simple plots were chosen. Once I did the Aesop fable "Lion and the Mouse" because it was only two characters but could be effective as a dance. Lion movements were large steps, with arms and hands (paws) moving with exaggerated large steps. The head moved menacingly side to side with each step. Mouse, of course, made tiny little steps as if scurrying from side to side. When mouse removes the thorn from the lion's paw, tiny picking movements were made with the hand, and then scurry, scurry, scurry. Lion's moves at the end were joyful steps celebrating his freedom rather than long menacing ones. Only once an attempt was made to present "Cinderella," with dance focusing only on the main character. At the beginning were sweeps and scrubs and washing clothes, representing

the drudgery of the girl's life. The entire offering was done to waltz
music. In the middle were swirls and beautiful waltz movements representing the change by the fairy godmother and attendance at the great
ball. That section ended with a limping step indicating the lost glass
slipper. The last segment went back to the sweeping, mopping, and
washing and the regular waltz happily at the end. This was only a mildly
successful presentation. A later dance designed to simulate the fable
about a battle between the sun and the wind received much more exciting responses. Arms and hands circling represented the sparkle of the
sun, and sweeps of arms and swirls of body for the wind were readily
imitated by children. The responding energy was far greater than the
reaction to the moody Cinderella portrayal.

The transition of these early trials into the development of *African and
African American Stories with Dance and Movement* came partly from reports from the experimental program in which I was involved. "A Is for
Africa" was a program I designed to help children in African American
communities and elsewhere learn about the beauty of Africa. One purpose was to encourage African American children to feel positive about
their African heritage. The development of African and African
American stories into dance began with "Anansi and the Bird Man" and
"Why the Sun and Moon Live in the Sky." Through those aforemen-
tioned reports of programming shared with others involved in outreach,
plus professional and community word of mouth, it was these presentations that gained popularity. Requests were received specifically for the
African and African American stories with dance and movement, which
were shared throughout the Los Angeles City Library's branches. Requests were also received from outside organizations. Therefore, there
began a focus on learning and developing African-based stories in dance.
I did not entirely give up on other varieties of stories and occasionally
tried other cultural presentations, but it was the African story presentations that were requested most, even in other ethnic communities.
   Soon it was apparent that African stories with animal characters and
actions were easy to visualize and probably were the best stories for this
kind of presentation. Also, with some investigation, I found that the
dance tradition in African included amateur creations. For the Ibos of
Nigeria, for instance, no distinction is made between professional and
amateur dances—everyone dances whether he is an accomplished dancer
or not. In fact, dancing is one activity in which everyone tries to excel
because on certain occasions in one's lifetime one just has to dance. Yet
not even the most accomplished dancer ever dreamed of turning professional in the context of the traditional community, for that would subject
him to as much ridicule as if he had confessed that he couldn't dance at
all.[4]

When I was called to teach in a library school program at the University of Wisconsin, Milwaukee, my assignment was teaching all courses for those planning to be children's librarians. Courses were designed to prepare librarians to become "urban specialists." In the storytelling course, my dance technique was passed on to students. A journalist from the local television station heard about the school's new program, interviewed me, and asked if my class would present our "storytelling with dance" on the local community television station. At first, I was elated; the library school program would receive more recognition in the community and the students would love it. Soon, I began to think that, being an American of African descent, could I *authentically* present African cultural content? The story to be presented was an African folktale with my dance interpretations. I called a male friend from Ghana and asked him to come to my apartment so we could discuss this matter. My concern was the possibility that the presentation by my students would be in any way an affront to the local African community. Upon demonstrating the "original" movements designed for the story, my friend exclaimed, "Who taught you that?" I asked what he meant, and he explained that every movement I had considered original was a familiar one from Ghanaian dance. He gave me the most important compliment I have ever received, saying, "All I can tell you is you are truly a Ghanaian woman!" He was so impressed that, instead of my telling the story, he wanted to narrate, while my students danced. After that, I added a few more stories with movement to my repertoire. In the foreword to my first edition of *Survival Themes in Literature for Children and Young People*, Jerome Cushman from UCLA wrote about my Los Angeles programs: "The project 'A Is for Africa' was a heritage experiment that preceded *Roots* by a few years. Several thousand children and adults have seen her interpretation of African folktales through narration music and dance."

From that time on, some aspect of movement or dance became a signature of most of my story presentations. There were plenty of opportunities to present a completely traditional program, but many requests were made specifically for inclusion of movement and dance. Following are descriptions and samplings of those specialized offerings:

- As I did in the first attempt at story with dance, there were times when I told the story and then turned on music, usually a portable player, and asked the audience to watch for the different motions representing the story or explained that they would see in my movements certain sequences of the story reenacted. At other times, I told stories while dancing, especially if battery packs were available for verbalizing during the movement. In such cases, music played in the background during the entire telling, although movement was not constant. "Once the sun" (sun movements), "and the moon" (moon movements), pause for verbal, "lived on the

earth just like the water" (water movements). "Sun" (sun movements), "and moon" (moon movements), "visited water often"
(with no water movements), and continuing this way, with intermittent dance representing the characters, combined with narrative
pauses.

- Many times, when telling "The People Could Fly," rhythmic movement without music introduced the story: "They say that long ago
the people could fly. The African people could fly, just step up on
the air and fly." At this point, with perfect quiet, steps on air are the
actions, and rhythmic flying movements are made, repeating the
opening phrases, after which the story about slavery continues.

- The presentation of "Thezin" in dance was not repeated many
times. This is the story from Haiti ending with the main character, a
little girl, sinking away in a kind of quicksand and dying in the end.
The dance steps for the early parts of the story were those of the girl
swinging a pail and scooping water from the lake where she goes to
draw water for the house. The body then moves, simulating the fish
Thezin. These steps were repeated to show many visits to the lake.
Depending upon the time allowed, prancing steps for the donkey
riding into market were added. Running steps added flavor, as the
girl seeks the fish that has been killed. The most trying part was the
expression of the main character's grief at the knowledge of Thezin's demise. Wrenching movements expressing grief were too
draining to repeat often. I decided that this story is effective enough
without the dance.

- Programs have been ended with the story titled "The Hat-Shaking
Dance," with my version of Anansi dancing and shaking his head
because stolen hot bananas are hidden under his hat. Children are
called upon to present their best hat-shaking dance, imagining that
they have a hat full of hot bananas on their heads.

- Children and adult audiences are introduced to poet Langston
Hughes by participating in reciting his "African Dance":

> The low beating of the tom toms
> The slow beating of the tom toms
> Low . . . slow—
> Slow . . . low—
> Stirs your blood
> A night veiled girl
> Whirls softly into a
> Circle of light
> Whirls softly . . . slowly
> Like a wisp of smoke around the fire
> And the tom toms beat,
> And the tom toms beat,
> And the low beating of the tom toms

Stirs your blood.[5]

The poem is done several times with beating of imaginary tom-toms or real drums. Groups of girls or individual volunteers whirl during the middle passage of the poem.

Ring games and singing games provide opportunities for movement. Traditional ring games like "Little Sally Walker" have an African American component at the end. The rhyme usually ends "Rise, Sally, rise and wipe our weeping eyes and turn to the east, my darling, turn to the west, my darling, turn to the one you love the best." Older African Americans will verify the version learned by many of them: "Put your hands on your hips and let your backbone slip, shake it to the east and shake it to the west, shake to the very one that you love the best." Then a replacement is picked by the person in the center of the ring. Younger ones love it in spite of such simple games being replaced by technological ones. A good source for this game and other chants for rhythmic play is Bessie Jones and Bess Lomax Hawes's *Step It Down: Games, Plays, Songs, and Stories from Afro-American Heritage* (New York: Harper and Row, 1972).

A staple in my story programs with African and African American themes is a chant from Ghana that I learned in the early 1970s. It speaks of the work of women, titled "Come to Dinner":

> First we go to hoe our garden, yah, yah, yah, yah.
> Then we carry jugs of water, yah, yah, yah, yah.
> Then we pound the yellow corn, yah, yah, yah, yah.
> Then we fill our pots with mush, yah, yah, yah, yah.
> Now we eat, come gather round the campfire, yah, yah, yah, yah.

Depending upon the setting of the story program, I use live or recorded drum music and together with the audience do rhythmic movements and dance to symbolize the actions in the chant: First line—alternate arms doing hoeing movements. Second line—steps in place with hands over head as if holding a bucket of water. Third line—alternate arms making pounding movements while moving the body rhythmically. Fourth line—alternate arms similarly but as if spooning into a large pot. Fifth line—now swing arms forward toward the mouth to simulate eating while still moving the body.

Another rhythm activity I have used frequently is "Cha Cha Kuli," pronounced "che, che koolay." I found it years ago in a book of Ghanaian singing games. Recently, several versions were found discussed on the Internet. This version appears in *The Dance of Africa* by Lee Warren with directions and illustrations[6]:

Cha Cha Kuli	Touch your head
Cha Cha Kofi Sa	Touch your shoulders

Kofi sa lange	Touch your waist
Cha Cha Hi lunga	Touch your knees
Cum adende	Come all the way down (touch your toes)

Each touch is done while shuffling feet side to side. The game repeats and gets faster and faster.

Seldom have there been one hundred or more children at one of the workshops on stories with movement, but it did happen once. In that case, I divided the children into groups and assigned them one character to work on together. When the story was narrated with music playing, each group danced their character in order of appearance. Their creations were quite good.

For the past ten years, with a standing invitation, I have prepared a Juneteenth program for the A. C. Bilbrew branch of the Los Angeles County Library. Young and old participate in one of the popular movements requested at each visit—the "Stomp Down Freedom" dance I coined after reading a slave narrative in which an old woman jumped up upon hearing the news of emancipation and did a stomp dance using these words:

> Stomp it down,
> Stomp it down
> Gonna stomp down
> freedom today

All types of communities have responded to the stories with movement. I was invited to do a performance at the Unitarian church called "the Onion" in the San Fernando Valley of Los Angeles. After presenting a story program at the church, a second invitation was received to do the storytelling and a movement workshop at the church's regional retreat, Camp de Benneville Pines. There, adults and young people participated in a workshop, learning to present stories with movement and to devise their own dances. The primary request was for African stories and dance.

It was a special pleasure to present stories and dance at the Village Theatre, a small theater in the African American community of Los Angeles. This was an opportunity to perform with all the accouterments of the theater, including an assistant piping in the music on cue from the fully equipped engineering area.

To illustrate the fun and rewards gained from the story-dance activity, one additional story follows:

A story program was being presented at The Egg and I on Wilshire Boulevard in Los Angeles, a large popular boulevard. The story was "Why the Sun and Moon Live in the Sky." The typical routine is I tell the story, with dance movements for sun, moon, and water. At the end, the children are asked to choreograph their own movements for those characters. We dance some of their creations. Finally, the children are told, "The dance movements come from my imagination. Now remember, water brought along all the water animals. Let's see how many water animals I can dance. If I can see them in my head, I can do a dance. Who is first?" The children call out "shark," "whale," "octopus," "turtle," "jellyfish," and the like, and I try a dance with the music. On this particular day, a boy about eight years old yelled, "Beaver!" Beaver had never before been requested, but quickly I thought to do step, step and bump, bump, bouncing my bottom to represent the beavers tale. This brought giggles. After the story hour was over and a few of us were left, someone called, "Come over here and look!" We all went to the plate-glass windows, where about six children were lined up going home down the sidewalk on Wilshire Boulevard—step, step, bump, bump, bouncing their little bottoms.

The rewards gained by these movement and dance activities is much, as Nikki Giovanni expresses in the last verse of her "Dance Poem":

> All you children gather round
> We will dance and we will whorl
> We will dance to our own song
> We must spin to our own world
> We must spin a soft Black song
> All you children gah round
> We will dance together[7]

NOTES

1. Lee Warren, *The Dance of Africa*, with dance instructions illustrated by Haris Petrie and photos by Vyvian D'estienne (Englewood Cliffs, NJ: Prentice Hall, 1972), p. 24.

2. Romain Goldron, *Ancient and Oriental Music* (New York: H. S. Stuttman, Doubleday, 1968), p. 42.

3. Goldron, *Ancient and Oriental Music*, p. 67.

4. Warren, *Dance of Africa*, p. 2.

5. Langston Hughes, "African Dance," in *Favorite Poems, Old and New*, by Helen Ferris (New York: Random House, 1957), p. 148.

6. Warren, *Dance of Africa*, p. 59.

7. Nikki Giovanni, *Spin a Soft Black Song* (New York: Hill and Wang, 1971).

III

Practical Uses and Resources

NINE

Suggestions for Educators, Parents, and Adult Leaders

> Children always needed stories to entertain them but they also needed tales to teach them how to act with one another, how to take care of the environment and what things to watch out for. —Nothando Zulu [1]

A few ideas for educators are suggested here as ways to begin using storytelling skills, varying classroom lessons, and adding benefits to learning. Many believe that the twenty-first century has become an "age of un-enlightenment" and that the first generation without stories and without an ability to concentrate has been spawned. Educators lament the absence of listening skills and a growing penchant toward violence among students young and old.

Throughout history, storytelling has held a central place in culture. We learned by comparing experiences, recognizing that response to the story is different from response to data. It is life's story patterns to which we respond. Some research claims that knowledge is organized by story-telling, but intermittingly stories have lost their value. Narratives will not solve all societal ills, but they can teach us to understand and speak some of the interior language of people and cultures. Memories and emotions are shared that can be likened to our own.

CALENDAR DAYS

With the object of sharing multicultural information and building respect for unfamiliar peoples and places, an easy method is celebrating calendar days with a selection of stories for special days of year. A large calendar posted on one wall of the classroom, home, or gathering place can reveal important days of celebration around the world. Those days, if selected

89

by a teacher, can be the storytelling moments of the classroom year. If a special day falls on a school holiday, the celebrating story time would be on a prior date. A useful title for beginning this project is *Guide to Celebrations and Holidays around the World* by Kathryn Matthew and Joy Lowe.

The following are some specific examples of special days.

Los Tres Reyes (Three Kings Day), or El Dia de Reyes

January 6 is a very special day in Mexico. It is the height of the holiday season, culminating in the twelve days of Christmas and the day of Epiphany celebrated for many years by Christians as the day of Jesus's baptism. In Mexico, the day commemorates the visit of the wise men or three kings to the site of Jesus's birth. Communities celebrate sometimes with parades, and children are given gifts on this day instead of Christmas. The holiday could be celebrated or mentioned in a story combined with narratives of festivals from other cultures held during December and early January.

Chinese New Year

Chinese New Year traditions differ in various parts of China. Some general traditions are the New Year's Eve dinner. This is the most important dinner of the year, usually a family dinner, gathering of family, or family reunion. Fish and dumplings for prosperity are served, and children may be given *red packets*, or envelopes with money, to suppress evil and to keep the children healthy.

In keeping with the focus on storytelling, there is the legend of a mythical beast called "Year" who appears on New Year's Eve night. He can harm people but is afraid of the color red, fire, and loud sounds. People shoot fireworks to fend off the evil of "Year," and they stay awake most of the night.

HINA MATSURI (DOLL FESTIVAL)

Although this is not a national holiday, many families set aside March 3 as the day to wish girls health and happiness. It is also called "momo no sekku" (Peach Festival) for the peach blossom season. This would be an appropriate time for a display of dolls and stories about dolls. A traditional display of dolls might be loaned by a Japanese family, which would include an arrangement of the dolls, with the emperor and empress dolls usually at the top and others in order below them. Libraries will have information about this display and traditional songs and games.

Sakura Matsuri (Cherry Blossom Festival)

The Sakuri Matsuri (Cherry Blossom Festival) dates back to the eighth century BC. More than a century ago, the Japanese government gave this country thousands of cherry blossom trees as a gift. In Washington, DC, the festival honoring this gift and offering a view of the trees is celebrated with a parade and many other festivities. In April, such other cities as New York and Monterey, California, which received trees from the 1912 Japanese gift, hold festivals each year.

Bear Dance Celebrations

Bear dance celebrations are held during the second week of June yearly by the Utes and other tribal nations. An opportunity is provided for students to learn about the bear, considered sacred in some cultures. From collections with some authenticity, bear stories can be told. Although Bear himself is sacred for some, it appears that many bear dance festivals are open to visitors from other cultures. Providing a small cultural awakening through story presentations is entirely possible.

Dragon Boat Festival

The Chinese Dragon Boat festival is a significant holiday in China and may be one with the longest history. It occurs on the fifth day of the fifth lunar month. Boat races are held, with all boats in the shape of dragons. Several legends about and related to the festival would be of interest for telling, or this may the time to tell any dragon stories available. For young children, drawing and building a dragon boat would be a pleasant classroom activity. *Dragons, Dragons, Dragons* by Helen Hoke, with pictures by Carol Barker, is a good source for stories.

Puerto Rican Day

Puerto Rican Day is celebrated with a huge parade in New York City and in other American cities. The second Sunday in June was established to celebrate the Puerto Rican cultural presence in the United States. This is seen as a day of empowerment for Puerto Ricans, to promote and recognize Puerto Rican achievements, and to promote community development on all levels. Stories by Pura Belpré, a Puerto Rican storyteller and writer, are popular.

Sun Dance

The summer solstice is the period of time for an approximately eight-day celebration called Sun Dance held by many of America's tribal nations. Because Sun Dance involves sacred rituals, imitations are not recommended. However, the theme would be appropriate for older students and adult audiences to learn about the special significance of these rituals and the historical action of the U.S. government in outlawing the Sun Dance (1904). There has been controversy about nontribal members who fatally tried to imitate sun lodge fasting rituals. However, teachers, leaders, and storytellers could give information, show films, and tell stories with the *sun* as the theme.

James Beckworth Days

In history courses about settlement of the West, in lesson plans about cowboys, and in affirmation of African American history or simply because this man's story is interesting, a biographical narrative could easily be shaped about James Pierson Beckworth. He was one of many cowboys and explorers of African descent, but Beckworth may be the only one known to have recorded his story of exploration. For years, little was recorded in history books or elsewhere about African Americans during the period of western exploration. Today there is more. In the Sacramento Valley of California, Beckworth Frontier Days are held during the first week of October, celebrating Beckworth's creation of a safe passage across the Sierra Mountains.

Dia de Los Muertos (Day of the Dead)

The Day of the Dead is a Mexican celebration of those departed. It is celebrated in the United States with special foods and representative rituals similar to those held in Mexico. There, the day is celebrated with parades, decorations near graveyards, and candies in the shape of skulls and skeletons. Many Americans find this a morbid way to deal with death, but others consider such a festival as a healthy way to face mortality and fears of death. Perhaps a storytelling program might be more readily accepted in a predominantly Mexican American community of students. If one dares, this would be good time for an adult story program designed to confront attitudes toward death. There are many stories from *all* cultures that could be used as a catalyst for discussion. Classroom teachers must determine their own comfort zones. The celebration is *real*, and the cultural references are *important*, and this is a perfect time for ghost stories.

Kwanzaa

Kwanzaa is a modern African American celebration originated in Los Angeles by Dr. Maulana Ron Karenga. The first celebration was held in 1966. Seven days of celebration from December 26 to January 1 are dedicated to *Nguzo Saba*, or seven principles. Derived from the Swahili phrase *matuna ya kwanza,* which means "first fruits," the ceremonies are rooted in harvest festivals held by many African tribes. Dr. Karenga hoped to establish a solid connection between African Americans and Africa. The design of the seven-day rituals also promotes family unity. A public, home, or school storytelling program might be designed to inform audiences about this special celebration but also to examine the seven principles through story. All the principles could be considered universal. Kwanza stories are now available, but any African American family stories would be appropriate.

Personal Note: Many holiday programs have been requested for schools and churches. The following program was presented for the city of Henderson, Nevada. A multicultural holiday program was requested for a citywide festival:

> "The Sandal Seller" — *Japanese New Year's story*
> "The Elves and the Shoemaker" — *Appropriate story for the Christmas holiday about giving and gratitude*
> "The Aztec Princess" — *Mexican story, also called "The First Ojo de Dios"*
> "Legend of the Black-Eyed Peas" — *African American story about the New Year and more; good for Kwanzaa*
> "David and the Monster in the Woods" — *A Hanukkah story*
> Hanukkah song
> Japanese Work Dance
> African Dance of Celebration

TELLING TALL TALES AND LEARNING ABOUT THEM

Tall tales provide access to history. Some of the characters in these larger-than-life legendary stories have a *real* place in history. Young and old are fascinated with such characters. Their charm is equal to that of comic book characters. Using this appeal, the leader can introduce more mundane historical information. One good source is *American Tall Tales* by Mary Pope Osborne. Stories for telling can be found at:
www.americanfolklore.net/folklore/tall-tales.
The following are examples of tall tale characters.

John Henry

With origins in West Virginia, John Henry was an ex-slave who after the Civil War worked for the Chesapeake and Ohio Railroads, drilling holes for rails to be laid. Along came a salesman touting the steam drill as faster than any man. A competition was held between John Henry and the steam drill. Just as the celebration of John Henry's win began, he dropped dead. There are statues in the area recognizing the strength and character of the "steel-drivin' man."

Johnny Appleseed

A number of stories have been written about Johnny Chapman and his desire and attempts to plant apple trees over the American landscape to insure against starvation. He roamed the wilderness, planting trees. His story is perfect for studies of ecology and the environment. Stories similar to *The Magic Apple* by Rob Cleveland could be told along with the biographical one of Chapman.

Paul Bunyan

Much has been written about the legendary lumberjack whose strength, speed, and skill surpassed all other humans. Many stories of his individual feats are entertaining. See *Paul Bunyan and His Great Blue Ox*, retold by Wallace Wadsworth and illustrated by Enrico Arno (Garden City, NY: Doubleday, 1964).

Pecos Bill

The stories about this charming but outrageous cowboy are obvious spoofs and designed for humor. Such names as "Slue-Footed Sue," the girl he loved, and the legend that the one and only time Pecos was thrown off a horse was in a Kansas tornado are samples of such exaggerations.

Mike Fink

Born somewhere around 1770 to 1780 at Fort Pitt (now Pittsburgh), this American keel boatman was known as the "king of the keelboaters." Keelboats were the main method of transportation and commerce during his times. His stories can link to lessons on the history of transportation and commerce in the United States.

Annie Oakley

From 1860 to 1926 was the lifetime of Phoebe Annie Oakley Mogee, known for her shooting skills. There are many tales of her performances with Buffalo Bill's Wild West Show. Her feats of marksmanship are said to be mostly true and exceptional for a woman of her times. She is the character celebrated in *Annie Get Your Gun* (1946), the Broadway show by Irving Berlin. Use Oakley's stories to spotlight women's contributions to the excitement of western settlement and for discussions of the evolving role of women.

Casey Jones

The "Ballad of Casey Jones" remains entertaining and is another that can be told while studying railroads. Jones's story is that of the Cannonball Express engineer with the reputation of never arriving late. In the end, Jones took too great a chance for the sake of time and told his assistant to jump, realizing that his passenger train would collide head on with an oncoming freight train.

Davy Crockett

Tennessee born in 1786, another folk hero, soldier, frontiersman, politician, and hunter, Crockett was known for his homespun humor and travels. Many stories about him could assist in historical discussions, including the fact that he was one of many *indentured servants* hired out and "bound" by contract. For stories, use the website http://americanfolklore.net/folklore/heroes-champions/.

GEOGRAPHY

Geography lessons can begin early by charting on a map or globe the places of a story's origin, including places around the world and regions of the United States. Foods of different parts of the world are also an easy topic to focus on with storytelling.

National Geographic operates websites devoted to lesson plans for teachers. Among the offerings, there are lesson plans that study stories from cultures around the world. An overview of one plan designed for grades 3 to 5 states,

> Students will examine stories and myths about ancient Egypt through time. First they will learn about the famous modern Egyptian myth about the "curse of the mummy." Then they will investigate ancient Egyptian culture and belief systems, including the influences of *geography* on the beliefs and customs of the time. They will then explore myths and stories from ancient Egypt. Finally, they will read about and discuss the influence of ancient Egypt and geography on modern culture.[2]

BIOGRAPHICAL STORIES

Biographical stories are available or can be written for almost all areas of study, including math. The spotlight on people allows educators committed to multicultural education an automatic method for inclusion. Often teachers are required to present the same historic figures each year. New biographical figures may add a bit of excitement and cultural variation.

The story of Bessie Coleman would add new flavor to discussions of early flight, which usually focus on the Wright brothers. The history of World War II is a good time to tell the story of Sequoyah and the code workers. There are hundreds of similar examples. Biographies written for children are often simple stories almost ready to be told.

Personal Note: For years, I have used the following biographical story of Rosa Parks as an example. Participants in storytelling workshops are asked to read it and, with their own background knowledge, tell it in their own way.

Rosa Parks

When Rosa Parks was a little girl growing up in Montgomery, Alabama, she hated the special rules that separated African Americans from those of European descent. People were called either "white" or "colored." Rosa was taught by her parents to be proud of herself and other African Americans who had contributed to the development of this country. After Rosa grew up and became a working woman, the rules of separation continued. On the city buses, if a white person needed a seat and a seat was available at the back of the bus, an African American person was required to move to the back and give the seat nearer to the front to the white person. Sometimes, African Americans were asked to stand and allow a Caucasian person to sit. On December 1, 1955, Rosa was riding home on the bus after a long day's work. She refused when asked by the bus driver to give her seat to a white man. For this, she was arrested and put in jail. African Americans in Montgomery decided to boycott all buses because of what happened to Rosa. Individuals and groups of African Americans all over the country supported their efforts. Dr. Martin Luther King Jr. later became leader of the boycott and other protests for the civil rights of African Americans. Finally, the Supreme Court of the United States declared that the bus company had to change its rules. Because of this incident, more actions were taken to remove unfair laws that applied to African Americans. We call all these actions the civil rights movement, and Rosa Parks is often referred to as the "Mother of Civil Rights."

TEACHING EARLY MATH

Cumulative tales have been used with the very young to have fun with addition. Children may shout out the totals after each participant appears or add up the number of participants. Using the story "Bremen Town Musicians," animals can be counted and added to the number of robbers, as one example. Older students might enjoy creating a math problem from a story.

ART AND ARTIFACTS

Personal Note: When presenting programs with emphasis on African stories, I have often brought my collection of small African musical instruments. Children love playing the thumb piano and the three-string lute if time is allowed.

Museum visits would be useful as way of interesting young people in myths. Many cave drawings and other artifacts are directly related to mythological stories. Some statues are of mythological figures.

Drawing a picture while telling a story may be fun for young aspiring artists. See Anne Pellowski's *Drawing Stories from around the World and a Sampling of European Handkerchief Stories*.

SCHEDULED STORY TIME

A scheduled time for reading aloud or telling tales can be a pleasing retreat for both students and leaders. There is usually excitement about classroom library visits and book-browsing experiences, and it is a safe assumption that children would look forward to a scheduled story time. A promise to read aloud or tell stories chosen by the children can provide incentive for children to read. Groups could be assigned to look at books together and choose story titles. From these choices, selected titles might be read aloud. It may seem that reading aloud is unrelated to storytelling, but reading aloud can substantially improve story learning and practice.

Today's young people are unfamiliar with classic rhymes of the past. A teacher might try some of them with older students, including those in high school. Explaining the origins of these rhymes and discussing the social meaning of rhymes originally written as adult satire could prove rewarding. An example would be discussing the social and economic meaning of the following:

> Sing a song of sixpence, a pocket full of rye
> Four and twenty blackbirds baked in a pie
> When the pie was opened the birds began to sing
> Wasn't that a dainty dish to set before the king?
> The king was in his counting house, counting out his money
> The queen was in the parlor, eating bread and honey
> The maid was in the garden, hanging out the clothes
> Along came a blackbird and nipped off her nose.

CREATING STORIES

Young people of elementary school age and up can create their own stories. Teamwork can be encouraged by having a group produce one story. A classroom story collection kept in a notebook could become a publication to take home. Older students might also be encouraged to write in order to understand the structure of stories and folklore. A helpful source is *Creative Storytelling: Choosing, Inventing, and Sharing Tales for Children* by Jack Maguire.

As a project, junior high school and high school students can learn to tell stories. The nearest elementary school could become a lab for presenting their stories. Some cities, such as Las Vegas, operate a storytelling initiative in the schools teaching the art of storytelling. An auditorium presentation for the public is given at the end of the year. Similar to a drama group's preparation of a play, participants learn storytelling methods and present stories. High school students might enjoy turning *classic tales into rap*. In *Children Tell Stories: A Teaching Guide* by Martha Hamilton and Mitch Weiss, step-by-step guides for teachers are offered.

Found on the Internet is *Cap O'Rushes: A Folkloric and Literature Resource for Teachers and Librarians*. Under the page "Fairy Tale Motifs," there is a project designed to teach young people about storytelling and to encourage them to write and tell tales. The project begins with a discussion of the oral nature of storytelling and looks at character motifs, such as villains, helpers, friends, and messengers. Place motifs include home, paradise, bad place, limbo, and more. Students are taught to chart stories and examine story content accordingly. The contact person for this course is Carole at cajs@rcn.com.

Don't forget the Public Broadcast System (PBS), both television and radio, as a source. In many areas, especially large cities, materials pertinent to storytelling will be found in the PBS store. There are also catalogs available. Tall tale segments about Pecos Bill and others have appeared there. Rosella Archdale, Hoskie Benally, Corbin Harney, and Tchin are storytellers from various tribal nations who have shared stories and information from their cultures. Some PBS story segments are found at http://pbskids.org.

CRAFTS

Making masks to represent story characters is a good project. This works especially well with African stories and stories from tribal groups in America. Use of masks is also a strong tradition of the Chinese and Japanese. Mask-making material can be as simple as a brown paper bag or could evolve into a story/art project producing artistic renderings for display. Myths are particularly potent stories for making masks. Many cultures use masks for the reenactment of their myths in various rituals. This would be an opportune time to also introduce dance by letting children, with guidance, choreograph dances for selected myths.

Make Ojo de Dios using popsicle sticks and knitting yarn. Instructions can be found in the local library. Today, the Ojo de Dios may be found in homes of people from many different cultures throughout the world. They are used as decorative art and as a good omen to bring blessings into the home. Examples have been found in Egypt and Africa as well as throughout the Americas. The Ojo de Dios has become a universal symbol for seeing and understanding the unseen.

To test retention, tell the story on one day and allow overnight for absorption. Discuss the story in the next day's class. The variations in retention and interpretation may be surprising. Have children tell the same story from the point of view of one of the characters: "I am Cinderella's stepsister," "I am the witch, and two children are nibbling on my house," or "I am a lion, and one day I met a little mouse."

Personal Note: It was a pleasure and privilege to be invited to a school for the deaf and a school for the blind in Los Angeles. Translators were no problem for the deaf children, and the children at the blind school were hearing, but the organizers at both the blind school and the school for the deaf wanted me to include story with dance, which I usually included in every program. At the blind school, I was told to simply describe what I was doing; the children would respond in their own way, and they did, but what about the children who were deaf? They could not hear the music. For that session, I did not have a live drummer as I did whenever affordable. Instead I used my boom box. The teacher advised me to tune the music to its loudest and place it on the floor. She placed an extra microphone near it. "Tune it with the highest bass," she told me. This way, these children could feel the vibrations when they placed their hand on the floor where all of them sat. What a grand time we had sharing stories and rhythms together!

Although the focus of a teacher-storyteller is developing language and improving verbalization, there is always the opportunity to blend storytelling with media. Popular movies may be shown, drawing young people to the subjects of fairy tales and folklore. Numerous folk- and fairy tales have been interpreted into movies and video, including *The Little Mermaid, Snow White, Little Red Riding Hood, Sleeping Beauty, Cinderella, Bluebeard,* and *The Princess and the Frog.* These could be shown during an annual storytelling festival sponsored by a school specializing in drama or a cooperative sister school. This offers an opportunity to discover and showcase area storytellers and student storytellers. Such activities will contribute to the community's appreciation of the arts.

Numerous books have been directed toward teachers and the use of storytelling in the classroom. Some of those are included in chapter 12.

NOTES

1. Nothando Zulu, in Eliana Gramer and Larissa Peifer, "Keeping the Oral Tradition Alive in Minnesota: Black Master Storytellers Festival," *Twin Cities Daily Planet,* (October 9, 2010).

2. "Ancient Egypt: Stories and Myths," *National Geographic Education*, 2013, available online at http://education.nationalgeographic.com/archive/xpeditions/lessons/06/g35/kingtut.html?ar_a=1.

TEN

Stories to Tell

Included in these notes and synopses are stories I have told or that are in my semiactive repertoire.

AESOP'S FABLES: MORALS AND PHILOSOPHY

Fables are wonderful filler material for a story program. The shorter ones can be used as introductions. Some of the longer ones, such as "The Hare and the Tortoise," still charm the young, and adults love giving their own interpretations to the morals. One of my favorites is "The Miller, His Son, and the Ass." A miller and his son were going to market. The two of them drove the ass, which was for sale. People passed them and made fun because they were walking when at least one of them could ride. The father had the boy get on the ass, and they walked along on their way, feeling very happy, when an old man met them, saying to the boy, "You lazy rascal! You ride and let your poor father walk!" Ashamed, the son got off the ass and insisted that his father ride. Not long after, they met another, who said, "How selfish that father is to ride and let his son walk!" Thinking he had solved the whole matter, the father took his son up on the ass with him. Then there came yet another who was more disgusted than the others, saying, "How dare the two of you ride on that poor little creature? You are much better able to carry it." Still wanting to do the right thing, father and son tied the donkey's legs to a pole, and both carried it on to the market. When they entered the market, they were a funny sight, and crowds gathered around them, laughing, pointing, and making much noise. The noise frightened the donkey, who kicked his legs loose, fell in the river, and drowned. The father said to his son, "We have lost the ass, but we have learned that when you try to please everyone, you please no one, not even yourself."

See Edna Johnson, Evelyn R. Sickels, Frances Clarke Sayers, and Carolyn Horovitz. *Anthology of Children's Literature*, 5th ed. (Boston: Houghton Mifflin, 1977).

ANANSI AND THE BIRD MAN: FRIENDSHIP

This story has been a continuing part of my active repertoire. It was one of the first stories I used with children in developing dance. Anansi, the Spider Man, and the Bird Man are friends. They play card games together, until one day when the Bird Man wins Anansi's favorite ring and flies away with it. Anansi sets out to get his ring back, enlisting the help of Tiger. Tiger plays dead so Bird Man will come to his funeral and Anansi can catch him. The plan is foiled, and Anansi tries other ruses. He uses his special powers and makes himself small enough to hide in Bird Man's nest, planning to make himself big again when Bird Man appears. Bird Man proves to be as smart as Anansi, and they decide to be friends again. The story can also be found under the titles "Anansi and Chim Chim" or "Annancy and Chim Chim," the latter being found in Pamela Colman Smith. *Annancy Stories*, available as an ebook at Amazon.com.

THE BAOBAB TREE: NATURE

This story explains why the baobab tree appears to be upside down. In the beginning of time, "when the stones were soft," the baobab tree had asked to be placed in the veld. The tree was not happy there and asked to be moved to the high plains. This placement did not please the baobab tree. When the third request for placement was made, the angry god placed the tree upside down. Today it grows with a huge trunk and a few branches and leaves at the top. These were once the tree's roots. From: Eleanor B. Heady. *When the Stones Were Soft: East African Fireside Tales*, illus. Tom Feelings (New York: Funk and Wagnalls, 1968).

THE BEAUTIFUL GIRL AND THE FISH: AFRICAN STORY

This is another version of "Nomi and the Magic Fish" and a tale called "Thezin," which I have told for years. A beautiful girl much sought after searches for a very handsome husband. One day she meets a man to her liking in the marketplace and asks him to marry her. The handsome male refuses, saying as much as he would like to have her as his wife, being not only man but a fish from the river at Idumaibo, he must return to river. The girl is so enamored that she marries him anyway with the agreement that she will come to the river and call for him by singing a magic song. Every day the girl visits the river and calls to her husband,

and they spend time together. It is her brother who discovers her secret and tells his parents. Her father, in anger, kills the fish and to punish his daughter serves it to her to eat. Her brother sings a song revealing that the fish is her chosen one. She runs to the river and cries out for her husband, and when the river turns red, she realizes that the worst has happened. Distraught, the beautiful girl jumps into the river and becomes a mermaid (onejegi). See Abayomi Fuja. *Fourteen Hundred Cowries and Other African Tales,* illus. Ademola Olugebefola (New York: Washington Square Press, 1973).

THE BEAUTIFUL GIRL IN THE MOON TOWER: FANCIFUL STORY OF LOVE

A son named Anton dreamed of a girl who placed a handkerchief over his face. When he told his mother about the dream, she said, "You dream of the girl who lives with her father in the tower of the moon." After helping the eagle, the ant, the lion, and the dove, Anton sets out to find the beautiful girl. Each of these animals provide him with the magic he needs to travel to the moon and find the father who keeps his daughter captive. His only recourse to marrying the beautiful girl is to kill the father. With her help he learns the secret of the father's life and kills him. He and the girl marry, and Anton becomes king of the inhabitants of the moon. The beautiful girl of the tower becomes his queen. This story is the first title found in the section called "Real, Extravagant, and Fanciful" in Virginia Hamilton. *The People Could Fly: American Black Folktales,* illus. Leo and Diane Dillon (New York: Knopf, 1985).

THE BIG TOE: GHOST STORY

This story is what several story tellers call a "jump tale," a scary tale that makes you jump at the end. There are several versions of the tale, which can be made scarier if you wish. In one version, a young boy picks up something that he thinks is fat meat, washes it, and throws it into the greens cooking on the stove. Later he is haunted by the sounds of someone calling, "I want my big toe!" The sound continues coming into the room and finally, "I got you!" This story is almost a replica of "Tailypo." In that one, as indicated in the title, the ghost loses his tail, and the calling pattern is much the same. Find "The Big Toe" in Alvin Schwartz. *Scary Stories to Tell in the Dark* (New York: Scholastic, 1989). An illustrated version of "Tailypo" is Joanne and Paul Galdone. *Tailypoe: A Ghost Story* (New York: Clarion, 1977).

THE BREMEN TOWN MUSICIANS: ANIMAL TALE

From Grimm's *Household Tales*, this cumulative story is detailed in chapter 6. A donkey leaves home to become a musician in Bremen Town. He meets an old dog, a cat, and a rooster, all of whom have become old and no longer valued. Together they chase robbers away from a house and steal the hiding place. There they decide to live out the rest of their lives using the fortune left by the robbers. See Edna Johnson, Evelyn R. Sickels, Frances Clarke Sayers, and Carolyn Horovitz.. *Anthology of Children's Literature*, 5th ed. (Boston: Houghton Mifflin, 1977).

BR'ER RABBIT BUILDS A HOME: TRICKSTER HUMOR

This tale of brother rabbit told by Jackie Torrance is found in *Jump Up and Say!* by Linda Goss and Clay Goss. All the creatures of the woods decided to get together and build a house for themselves. Br'er Rabbit got himself a ruler, stuck a pencil behind his ear, and scurried around busily, pretending he was working. The other animals worked hard and built the house.

When the house was finished, Br'er Rabbit chose the room upstairs and slipped in a shotgun, a cannon, and a big tin tub. His plan was to use these to scare the other animals away, leaving him alone with the house to himself. His last caper was to yell downstairs and ask the others, "When a big feller like me takes a chew of tobacco and wants to spit, where is he supposed to spit?" They answer, "Spit where you please." Rabbit yells, "Look out down there!" He turns over the tub he has filed with water, which comes rolling down the stairs. The animals takes off running. Rabbit locks the doors, closes the windows, and goes to bed like he owns the world. See Linda Goss and Clay Goss. *Jump Up and Say! A Collection of Black Storytelling* (New York: Simon and Schuster, 1995).

BROTHER WOLF SAYS GRACE: ANIMAL TALE

Brother Rabbit has been getting very lonesome hiding from the wolf. He loves Miss Fox. One day he decides to take a chance and dresses up for a visit to see Miss Fox. On the way, he is very careful, watching for any sign of the wolf, and he arrives safely at Miss Fox's house. They sit on the porch, courtin' a bit, and the time passes fast. Before he knows it, dusk is falling, and Brother Rabbit realizes he better get home fast. He says his goodbyes and starts the trip home. Soon he discovers a large box in the middle of the road that contains "sparrer grass" (asparagus). Brother Rabbit dearly loves "sparrer grass" and decides to eat some. He eats his way to the bottom of the box, where Brother Wolf is waiting. Making Brother Wolf say grace is the way rabbit escapes. Find in many collections of "Uncle Remus" tales, preferably newer or revised versions. Joel Chandler Harris. *Favorite Uncle Remus Tales* (New York: Houghton Mifflin, 1948).

COYOTE FIGHTS THE SUN: HUMOR, THE SUN, CULTURAL

When spring arrives, Coyote tells his daughter to throw out all the winter food and gather spring vegetables and greens. As it sometimes happens in the area of Mount Shasta, there is a brief show of spring, and the winter snows return. Coyote and family are left with no food. Instead of realizing his mistake, Coyote blames the sun, which he tries to shoot with his bow and arrow. Find this story in Mary J. Carpelan. *Coyote Fights the Sun: A Shasta Indian Tale* (Berkeley, CA: Heyday Books, 2002).

THE CREATION OF THE WORLD: CREATION STORIES

This wonderful, lyrical creation tale is perfect for a program of "creation stories" from various cultures. Before creation began, there was only the one who contains everything, Awonawilona; there was only blackness and nothingness. Awonawilona created life within himself with mists of growth streaming from him. He made light, the sun, and the mists condense and fall as water becoming the sea. While the world floated in the sea, forming seeds within himself, Awonawilona impregnated the waters, from which came the earth, mother of Four Directions, and Sky Father, covering everything. Gradually all things were created, including men, who were divided in six groups. Yellow, brown-grey, red, white, black, and all colors mixed. Men did not appear as they do today; they were strange creatures.

This is a very long myth, with explanations of the development of man, but it can be condensed and told in part as done here. Find this in Cottie Burland and Paul Hamlyn. *North American Indian Mythology* (London: Hamlyn, 1965).

CUPID AND PSYCHE: MYTHICAL LOVE STORY

Psyche, the youngest of the king's three daughters, excelled her sisters in looks and every other aspect. Men journeyed from far and near just to get a glance of her beauty. Her looks were so compelling that the goddess Venus was forgotten and ignored. She called upon her son, Cupid, for help, ordering Cupid to make Psyche fall in love with the vilest male available. This he might have done had she not shown Cupid a picture of Psyche. Even the god of love was not immune to Psyche's charms. Because Cupid said nothing to his mother, Venus assumed he would soon bring about Psyche's ruin. But Psyche fell in love with no one. Men were still content just to catch a glimpse of her. Venus made many efforts to bring Psyche to ruin, even bringing injury to Cupid, who loved Psyche. In the end, Cupid is healed of his wounds and returns to save Psyche. He calls a full assembly of the gods and announces to all, including Venus, that he will be married and immortality will be bestowed upon his bride. Love (Cupid) and Soul (Psyche) would remain together forever. (This story is essentially the same as "East of the Sun and West of the Moon," without the gods). Find the story in Edith Hamilton. *Mythology* (New York: Little, Brown, 1942).

THE DEVIL'S TRICK: A JEWISH FOLKTALE: HANUKKAH TALE

A short tale about the meaning of Hanukkah finds David alone with his baby brother on the first night of Hanukkah. Father had gone to the village to buy corn, and mother followed. After three days, David worries, and leaving the baby safely tucked in, he goes out to search for them. The devil whips up a storm, and unable to see, David tries to return home. When all seems lost, he sees the light of the Hanukkah candle and follows it home. The devil, who follows him home, tries to enter. David is just enough ahead to slam the door, catching the devil's tail. The devil promises to bring back his father and mother if David will release his tail. David starts to cut off the tail with an ax but instead singes it with the candle before opening door for his parents. "Remember, Hanukkah is no time for making trouble," David says. Find this story in Isaac Bashevis Singer. *Zlateh the Goat and Other Stories* (New York: Harper and Row, 1966).

THE DRAGON'S TEARS: JAPANESE, CULTURAL

In a deep mountain cave somewhere in a country faraway, there lived a dragon whose eyes shone in the darkness. The people often talked about the dragon. One thought he was beautiful; another said, "Someone should kill him." All the children were afraid of the dragon except one little boy, who wanted to invite the dragon for his birthday. The boy stole off, climbed to the mountain cave, and invited the dragon to his party. Being so pleased that someone thought kindly of him, the dragon began to cry. The dragon cried until his tears became a river. "Come climb on my back. I'll give you a ride home," he said to the boy. During the trip, a magical transformation took place, and the boy found himself riding home as the captain of a great dragon steamboat. Find this story in Florence Sakade. *Urashima Taro and Other Japanese Children's Stories* (Rutland, VT: Charles E. Tuttle, 1959).

DRAKESTAIL: IMPORTANCE OF FRIENDS

Both a cumulative tale and a beast tale, this classic still has charm. Drakestail the duck is very small but very smart. He has accumulated much wealth. Hearing of this, the king, who has fallen on hard times, borrows money from Drakestail. After a time of still not being repaid, Drakestail sets out to confront the king. Drakestail cumulates several friends and companions on his way, asking each to make itself small and climb into his liver. When the king attempts to rid himself of his lender, one by one Drakestail calls forth his friends from his liver, the last being the wasps, who sting the king until he his dead. Drakestail becomes king. Find this story in Andrew Lang. *The Red Fairy Book* (New York: Longmans, 1947).

EAST OF THE SUN AND WEST OF THE MOON: POVERTY TO RICHES

A beast tale similar to several others, this story is about a family whose father is very, very poor. He has many children—too many to feed. The prettiest is the youngest daughter. Along comes a white bear, who promises the man great riches in exchange for his youngest daughter. Convincing the daughter this will be of benefit to all, the girl agrees to leave with the bear. She rides on the back of the bear to a great castle. When the girl began to get lonely for her family, the bear (man) allows her to go home for a time with the promise that she would not tell her mother anything. Arriving home, she finds the family in a fine house. As predicted, her mother entices her into telling her that at night a man comes to lie in the other bed in her room. Mother gives her daughter a candle to light when the man comes into her room. Doing this causes the bear (man) to be banished to the place "east of the sun and west of the moon" where the stepmother who bewitched him lives. A series of events lead the princess to the faraway place, and eventually the prince is freed from his curse. Find this story in Edna Johnson, Evelyn R. Sickels, Frances Clarke Sayers, and Carolyn Horovitz. *Anthology of Children's Literature*, 5th ed. (Boston: Houghton Mifflin, 1977).

THE ELVES AND THE SHOEMAKER: HOLIDAY STORY

From Jacob and Wilhelm Grimm's *Household Stories*, a classic fairy tale is told that is often used during holiday seasons. A shoemaker and his wife have fallen on hard times, and all that is left is leather for one pair of shoes. The elves appear at night, bringing the gift of superior shoemaking and leather for more shoes. Thankful that someone has come to their rescue, the husband and wife watch and see their benefactors. They observe the naked elves, and the cobbler's wife decides to make them some fine clothes. Feeling quite dandy in their new clothes, the elves leave, never to return, but the man and wife are quite rich, and the shoes are in demand far and wide. Find this story in Jacob and Wilhelm Grimm. *Household Stories* (New York: Macmillan, 1886).

FIRST TEARS: AN INUIT TALE

A short simple tale is related about the day when man hunted seal for his family to eat. With joy he discovered many seals gathered by the water. As he crept toward them, they became restless and slipped into the water. One seal was left, but when man crept toward it, the last seal slipped away. This is when man felt water coming from his eyes and a strange sound coming from his throat. The water from his eyes tasted salty. Hearing man's cry, woman and boy came running, and after hearing man's story of all the seals escaping, those two found the water flowing from their eyes. This is the way people learned to weep. This Inuit tale is also called "How Man Learned to Cry." Find this story retold by S. E. Schlosser. "The First Tears: An Inuit Tale," *American Folklore* at:
americanfolklore.net/folklore/2010/09/the_first_tears.html.

THE FISHERMAN AND HIS WIFE: GREED

Also from Grimm's *Household Stories*, this story's theme is a familiar one in folktales around the world; the person or persons who find good fortune become so greedy that they seek more and more. This is the story of the fisherman's wife, who tests good fortune too many times. See Jacob and Wilhelm Grimm. *Household Stories* (New York: Macmillan, 1886).

THE FLEA: SPAIN, HUMOR, CULTURAL

Who would believe that the hide of flea was material stretched to cover cymbals? Who would believe that the hide of a flea was stretched to cover a tambourine? A king devises an extraordinary scheme to form the riddle:

> Belita—Felipa—they dance well together—
> Belita, Felipa; now answer me whether
> You know this Felipa—animalita
> If you answer me right, then you marry Belita
> The one who could solve the riddle . . .

See Ruth Sawyer. *Picture Tales from Spain* (New York: Lippincott, 1936). Find this story also in Edna Johnson, Evelyn R. Sickels, Frances Clarke

Sayers, and Carolyn Horovitz. *Anthology of Children's Literature*, 5th ed. (Boston: Houghton Mifflin, 1977).

THE FLUTE PLAYER: APACHE FOLKTALE

This poignant tale of a young brave who plays the flute beautifully ends sadly. The brave's sweetheart loves him and his music. When he leaves for the hunt and does not tell the girlfriend, she becomes ill, thinking that the man she loves has forgotten her. She dies, and upon his return, the warrior plays the flute at her grave. The sound of the flute can still be heard as the wind whistles through the canyons. Find this story in Michael Lacapa. *The Flute Player: An Apache Folktale* (Flagstaff, AZ: Northland [Rising Moon] Publishers, 1990).

GEMINI, THE TWINS: BROTHERLY LOVE, MYTH

Myths relating to astronomy can be long, complex, and involved, but one simple story is that of the twin brothers Pollux and Castor. Pollux was immortal, while Castor was mortal. The twins fell in love with two beautiful sisters who were already betrothed. Castor and Pollux challenged the other suitors to battle for the prize of the two maidens. Castor and Pollux won the battle, but Castor was seriously wounded and died. Pollux, overcome by grief, attempted to kill himself and join his brother in the shadow of Hades. Because he was immortal, Pollux could not kill himself and asked Jupiter to help him die. Impressed with the strength of brotherly love, Jupiter compromised, allowing the two to spend half of the day together in Hades and half in daylight. Jupiter also rewarded the devotion of Pollux by placing the immortal souls of the twins as brilliant stars close together in the sky. This is from Peter Lum. *The Stars in Our Heavens* (New York: Pantheon, 1948).

GIFT HORSE: LAKOTA STORY, CULTURAL

Flying Cloud is eager to prove himself as a hunter and to become a warrior. He goes on a four-day vision quest where he becomes closer to his horse, Storm, a gift from his father. It is the horse that helps him to achieve warrior status. Find this story in S. D. Nelson. *Gift Horse: A Lakota Story* (New York: Harry N. Abrams, 1999).

HE LION, BRUH BEAR, AND BRUH RABBIT:
AFRICAN AMERICAN FOLKTALE

The small animals are disturbed by He Lion, who roams around the forest, repeating out loud, "Me and Myself" over and over again. Frightened, the small animals seek the help of Bruh Bear, who keeps his distance from the lion but confronts him about his boasting. The lion declares himself king of the forest. Bruh Rabbit declares that man is the real king of the forest. He Lion, having never seen man, thinks this is false. When he finally meets man and is shot at, He Lion has to run and hide. He Lion still repeats his words but not so loudly in respect for man. The words are now "Me, Myself, and Man." This story is from Virginia Hamilton. *The People Could Fly* (New York: Knopf, 1985).

HOW GLOOSKAP FOUND THE SUMMER:
ALGONQUIN LEGEND, CULTURAL

This is an Algonquin legend from long ago when the people called themselves Wawaniki (Children of the Light). Glooskap was their kind leader, who did many great deeds. Once when it grew extremely cold, Glooskap set out to save the people, who were dying from the cold and lack of food. He traveled north, where he found the great giant called Winter. Glooskap entered Winter's wigwam and smoked a pipe with his host. Charmed by Winter, Glooskap slept for six months. The tale bearer, Loon, came, telling Glooskap about a land to the south where Summer lived and it was always warm. Glooskap left to find summer and save his people. He sang a magic song that whales obey, and a whale appeared and carried Glooskap south on the ocean. After an encounter with his friend the whale, the whale beached itself, but Glooskap pushed it out into the ocean and traveled inland. There he found a beautiful woman called Summer. He caught Summer and took her to meet Winter. Summer proved stronger than Winter, whom she gave all land to the north. She promised Winter he could have six months to rule the land and then she would return and reign, and that's the way it has always been. This story is from Charles Leland. *Algonquin Legends of New England; or Myths and Folklore of the Micmac, Passamaquoddy and Penobcot Tribes* (New York: Houghton Mifflin, 1884). The entire text of this title can be found at www.sacredtextx.com/nam/ne/al/al02.htm

HOW MAUI FOUND THE SECRET OF FIRE:
POLYNESIAN, CULTURAL

This story of Maui the trickster considers the origins of fire. Being inquisitive, Maui wondered about the source of fire. Maui poured water on the available fire and was scolded and sent to the volcano to get more. There he is given fire by Mahuika, the keeper of fire. Maui is still dissatisfied, not knowing the source. He throws his starter flame into the water and goes back to the volcano repeatedly, each time hoping to discover the source. Mahuika becomes angry when there is just one flame left. The two fight over that flame. Mahuika throws the source of fire into the Kaikamako tree. Maui figures out that if he rubs the wood of the tree together, fire will appear, and it did. See Suelyn Chin Tune. *How Maui Found the Secret of Fire*, illus. by Robin Yoko Burningham (Honolulu: University of Hawaii, 1991).

HOW THE EARTH WAS PEOPLED: AFRICAN TALE, CULTURAL

This selection from the Ngombe people seems more appropriate for adults. It would be a good choice for discussion and comparison to other myths about man's origins. Some would consider the marriage of brother and sister in the story incestuous, but these were the only two who could propagate the earth. Later the sister meets Ebenga, a very hairy man. She shaves him and has his child. This child was the source of witchcraft and evil. The brother and sister had more children, but evil was always present. This story is from Susan Feldmann. *African Myths and Legends* (New York: Dell, 1963).

JACK AND THE BEANSTALK: HUMOR, POVERTY TO RICHES

"Jack and the Beanstalk" is a classic droll. Jack trades the cow he is taking to market for five magic beans and is severely scolded by his mother. The beans are indeed magic and produce a beanstalk, which leads Jack to the house of the ogre in the sky. His three trips to the ogre's house produce wealth for him and his mother. Find this story in Joseph Jacobs. *English Fairy Tales* (New York: Putnam, 1892).

JACK AND THE DEVIL: EVIL VERSUS GOOD, HUMOR, APPALACHIAN

In some Jack tales, the character of Jack can be very lovable, but in this one he is a scoundrel. He is mean, beats his wife, and stays drunk. He has been told many times that, if he doesn't better himself, he will end up in hell. He finally dies and encounters the devil, but Jack is smarter than the devil and on three occasions manages to get a reprieve from hell by tricking the devil. When he finally arrives at the door of Hades for the last time, the devil doesn't want him! He gives Jack two live coals to find his way in his travels through darkness. The story ends. If at night, you see two lights swinging along in the dark and they don't seem to belong to anybody, that could be Jack! Adult audiences are those to whom I choose to tell this story, although I had a request from one preacher to tell it at his church. Find this story in Richard Chase. *Jack Tales* (New York: HMH Books for Young Readers, 2003). A different version of the same theme follows.

JACK, MARY, AND THE DEVIL: EVIL VERSUS GOOD, CULTURAL, JOHNS ISLAND

In this version of the tale, Jack is Mary's brother. Mary becomes enamored with a young man, who is really the devil. He asks to take Mary out. Her mother agrees. Jack asks if he can accompany them, but Mary refuses, saying Jack is too young. Her brother has unusual powers and is unusually smart. He follows the devil's buggy, and when Mary and her beau enter a store, Jack turns into a gold ring. His sister sees the ring and likes it. The devil buys it and takes Mary to his home wearing the ring (her brother Jack). When Mary realizes she is in hell, she wishes she had let Jack come along. He uses magic to turn back into himself and tells Mary he will help her escape. Then he turns himself into a ring again. When the two begin to escape, the rooster alerts the devil. Jack outwits the devil's bull by dropping magic grains of corn he brought along in his pocket. The brother and sister finally escape. The story is written in "gullah" language and has rhymes to be sung during the telling. This version is found in Guy and Candie Carawan. *Ain't You Got a Right to the Tree of Life? The People of Johns Island, South Carolina—Their Faces, Their Words, and Their Songs* (New York: Simon and Schuster, 1966).

THE JOLLY TAILOR WHO BECAME KING: POLAND, HUMOR

From Poland comes the tale of the merry little tailor named Mr. Nitechka. Mr. Nitechka was so thin that he could eat nothing but noodles, but he was happy and very handsome, especially when he braided his beard. His life changed when he used his sharp needle to sew up the foot of a gypsy woman who stopped in his place after cutting her foot. She told him that, if he left on Sunday and walked westward, he would come to a place where he would become king. Nitechka laughed at first but then began to dream of being rich and fat. He started his travels west, eventually making friends with Scarecrow, who joined him in his travels. They encounter a house in which the devil lives with his daughters. They are captured and seek a way to escape. Nitechka sings a song about the Virgin Mary, which provides forces that release them. On they travel to the town of Pacanow, where there has been constant rain since the king died. The princess promises to marry anyone who can stop the rain.

Nitechka promises to find a solution. He discovers that, when the king died, a hole was left in the sky. With the help of his friend Scarecrow, the townspeople, many ladders, and sharp needles, the tailor repairs the sky. He marries the princess. Scarecrow is appointed the great warden of the kingdom, scaring the birds away from the king's face. This story is found in Edna Johnson, Evelyn R. Sickels, Frances Clarke Sayers, and Carolyn Horovitz. *Anthology of Children's Literature*, 5th ed. (Boston: Houghton Mifflin. 1977).

LEGEND OF THE PALM TREE: BRAZIL, CULTURAL

The Legend of the Palm Tree was awarded a prize by the Children's Literature Committee of the Ministry of Education. The book was published in order to familiarize the children of Brazil with the folklore of the country. The female spirit of the palm tree steps out and gives instructions that will save the starving. Information is given for using various parts of the tree—the palms, the wood, and the palm nuts—establishing the importance of the palm tree in the lives of the people. See Matgarida Estrela Bandeira Duarte. *Legend of the Palm Tree*, illus. Paolo Werneck (New York: Grosset and Dunlap, 1940).

LOVE LIKE SALT: MEXICO, CULTURAL

From Mexico is the story of a king who had three daughters. When asked by the king to describe how much they love him, the youngest answers, "I love you like salt." The king is outraged and orders her put to death. He wants proof from the executioner by way of her eyes and one finger. The servant carrying out the order releases the girl, taking back a dog's eyes, but the daughter has to sacrifice one finger. She is found in a cave by a young prince, who falls in love with her. After taking her home, his parents arrange a big wedding. On the day of the festivities, the girl sees her father is present. The servants are told not to put salt in the food where he sat. The king, her father, complained, "Where is the salt? This food has no flavor. You can't eat without salt." The girl reminds him of his anger when she said, "I love you like salt" and tells him she is his daughter. When her father refuses to believe her, she shows him the hand with one missing finger. The king begs for forgiveness and holds eight days of feasting to honor his daughter. (In the version I like, it ends with "I was there, and they made me eat pig's feet.") Find this story in John Bierhorst. *Latin American Folktales* (New York: Pantheon, 2002).

THE MAGIC APPLE: MIDDLE EAST, CULTURAL

Three brothers set out to fulfill their father's dying wish for them to find happiness and riches. Each takes a separate path, goes to distant lands, finds treasures, and learns the true meaning of giving. Find this story in Rob Cleveland. *Magic Apple: A Folktale from the Middle East* (Atlanta, GA: August House, 2006).

A MAGIC PAINTBRUSH: THE STORY OF MA LIANG: GREED

A classic Chinese tale about a young man named Ma Liang, who was very poor. He helped a rich man tend cattle, and he loved to draw pictures. In a dream, an old man gave Ma Liang a paintbrush and told him to use it to help the poor. Whatever was drawn with the brush came alive. When people needed water, he drew a river, and the river appeared. When land needed plowing, he drew a cow to help. The jealous rich man contrived to throw Ma Liang into jail so that the magic brush could be stolen, but when the thief tried to use the brush, nothing happened. The rich man sent for Ma Liang, asking him to draw pictures that would come alive in exchange for being released from jail. Ma Liang agreed, having his own plan. "I will help you if you obey my words," he said. The jealous rich man expressed his wish for a golden mountain where he could always gather gold. Ma Liang drew the mountain but placed it across the sea. He drew a ship for the rich man's travel. The greedy man and many greedy followers climbed on board and started the trip to the mountain. Ma Liang drew a big wave that sank the ship and all aboard. A beautiful hardcover book version with a slightly different title but the same story is *Ma Lien and the Magic Brush*. See M. J. York. *The Magic Paint Brush* (New York: M. J. York Hardcover Books, 2012).

THE MIRROR OF MATSUYAMA: JAPANESE, CULTURAL

This classic Japanese tale is refreshing because it is one of the few with a wicked stepmother who changes in the end. On her death bed, a mother bequeaths a mirror to her daughter, saying "When you were still a young child, your father brought me this treasure. This I give to you before I die. After I am gone, if you become lonely, take out the mirror and in it you will see me." Her father remarries, and soon, the new stepmother observes her stepdaughter having moments alone with the mirror. She believes the child is planning to do her ill. The truth is eventually revealed, and the stepmother apologizes. The father, daughter, and stepmother become a happy family. See Yei Theodora Ozaki. *The Japanese Fairy Book* (Rutland, VT: Charles E. Tuttle, 1970). Full text of a long version of the tale can be found online at *World of Tales: Stories for Children, Folktales,*

Fairy Tales and Tales around the World at www.surlalunefairytales.com/books/japan/ozaki.html

MOLLIE WHUPPIE: FEMALE HEROINE

Mollie is one of the few female heroines in early folktales. She outwits the giant who lives across the "bridge of one hair," too small for him to cross. After being banished from their home because of poverty, Mollie and her sisters have three opportunities to become married to royalty. They must respond successfully to three requests of the king. Each feat requires a trip across the "bridge of one hair" and bringing back wares from the giant. Mollie accomplishes all three feats. This is one story that I have told often but have changed some of the violence at the end. When Mollie arranges for the giant to mistake his own daughters for herself and her sisters, the daughters are killed. I simply say, "Who knows what he did to those daughters?" At the end, the giant beats his wife to death, thinking it is Mollie. I change the ending saying, "She tricked the giant's wife, and Mollie made her final escape." Find this story in Joseph Jacobs. *English Fairy Tales* (New York: Putnam, 1892).

MR. SAMPSON CAT: BEAST TALE

Mr. Samson Cat and Widow Fox decided to live together. One day when Mr. Cat went out for walk, Rabbit came running and jumped on top of him. Mr. Cat growled ferociously. Rabbit told Wolf, "When I was running past Widow Fox's house, a beast jumped on me. I thought he was going to swallow me alive." The scene is followed by a series of very funny events, all of which convince the animals that Mr. Samson Cat is really a powerful beast. Find this story in Tasha Tudor. *The Tasha Tudor Book of Fairy Tales* (New York: Grosset and Dunlap, 1980).

THE PANCAKE: CUMULATIVE, HUMOR

Young ones still love this cumulative tale, also told as "The Gingerbread Boy." Using some of the terms from the Danish version, there was a *goody* who had seven hungry children. She was frying a pancake for them. Each of the seven plead for their share, beginning with terms like, "Oh, darling mother," the second, "Oh, darling good mother," and each of the seven improving on the others, ending with, "Oh darling, pretty, good, nice, clever, sweet mother." The goody chides them to wait until the pancake turned itself, and they could have a taste. The pancake turns itself, becomes firm, jumps out of the pan, and runs away. Mother runs after the pancake with the frying pan in hand, followed by her husband and seven children yelling for the pancake to stop. The pancake rolls by a man, who asks it to stop so he can eat. (The responses are especially enjoyed by young children.) "I have given the slip to Goody Poody and the goodman and seven children. I may well slip through your fingers Manny Panny." And so it is when the pancake meets Henny Penny, Cocky Locky, Ducky Lucky, Goosey Poosey, and Gander Pander. It is the pig who finally outwits the pancake and eats it. Find this story in Peter Asbjornsen. *Tales of the Field*, trans. by G. W. Dasent (New York: Putnam, 1908), and in other more recent collections.

THE PEOPLE COULD FLY: AFRICAN FOLKTALES

Even if they don't quite understand the meaning of slavery and freedom, children identify with the desire to fly. This story can be told at African American celebrations, used as an introduction to discussions of slavery, or told as part of a program without introduction. It begins, "They say the people could fly," immediately capturing the audience's imagination. The story has power that appeals to most audiences. After descriptions of the plight of slave workers, the old man who remembers the magic of flying and has taught some of the slaves the magic words gives the signal that it is time to use their power and leave. They climb up on the air and fly. This is the title story in one of Virginia Hamilton's collection of African American folktales. See Virginia Hamilton. *The People Could Fly*, illus. Leo and Diane Dillon (New York: Knopf, 1985).

THE RABBIT AND THE PARTRIDGE: AFRICAN AMERICANS, JOHNS ISLAND

This story is from the book, *Ain't You Got a Right to the Tree of Life?* where I found the "Jack" tale "Jack, Mary, and the Devil" described earlier. For young children, I alter the end of the story, but I like it because it is one in which the rabbit does *not* win. It begins, "Everybody think the rabbit got so much sense, but one day the partridge outsensed the rabbit." On that day, the partridge went out to walk and returned home with his head under his wing. He stopped at Rabbit's house and asked, "How you like my head?" Rabbit said, "I like it fine. Where is your head?" Partridge answered, "You old fool rabbit, I leave my head home for my wife to shave." Rabbit takes off, runs home, and tells his wife to cut off his head. When she refuses and argues against it, he says, "I won't die, 'cause Partridge cut his head off. He leaves it home for his wife to shave. Now I don't see why you can't cut off mine." Rabbit's wife finally gives in, takes a knife out of the drawer, and cuts off Rabbit's head. The wife goes to Partridge and scolds him, saying, "Why did you do that? Why did you tell Rabbit you left your head home for your wife to shave, when all the time you had it hidden under your wing?" Partridge said, "Well you sure ain't no fool. We ought to get along." After that Partridge had two wives: his and Rabbit's wife.

(For young children, I start the cut, and Rabbit screams and runs to patch up the wound. Wife scolds Partridge, and Partridge answers. "You sure ain't no fool. If you ever get tired of that fool rabbit, I'll marry you. Two wives is better than one.") See Guy and Candie Carawan. *Ain't You Got a Right to the Tree of Life? The People of Johns Island, South Carolina— Their Faces, Their Words, and Their Songs* (New York: Simon and Schuster, 1966).

RICE FROM THE ASHES: ARGENTINA, CULTURAL

From Argentina comes a story with strong similarities to "Cinderella." A young girl's mother died, and her father remarried a woman with two daughters of her own. The husband's daughter was made the house servant. She had only a little lamb to keep her company. One day the stepmother orders the servant girl to slaughter the lamb. The only way the lamb would be saved was if she could separate rice that had fallen in the hearth from ashes. A dove came to her aide and separated the rice while she slept. The stepmother contrived other seemingly impossible feats as the price for the lamb—separating stones from lentils, sugar from ashes, and spinning two bags of wool into thread. The stepmother finding one wisp of thread left over ordered the lamb killed. Before going to slaughter, the lamb told the stepchild, "Inside me you will find a small cup. Remove it and keep it always." The lamb was slaughtered, and she found the cup. An old man came along and asked for a drink. She gave him one from the cup. As it happened, the two stepsisters acquired lambs and had the same experience, except when the old man (God) appeared they refuse him a drink of water. In town was the king, whose wife, the queen, had died. Before dying, she told her son, the prince, that he would marry a girl with a cup of gold. Word spread that the prince is seeking this person. The stepmother tried to fool the prince, telling him it was her oldest daughter. He discovered this was not true, and the younger stepsister attempted to be the one but did not succeed. Finally with the help of a songbird, the prince discovered the servant girl and found that she had a golden cup. The two young people rode off to the palace and wed. This story is in John Bierhorst. *Latin American Folk Tales* (New York: Pantheon, 2002).

THE RUG MAKER: AFRICAN TALE ABOUT WORK, CULTURAL

Here is an African story about the necessity to learn a trade. The chief has tried to encourage his son to learn a trade, but the young man, Kamalo, asks for more time to hunt and play before making a commitment to study. When the boy meets a young girl in the forest gathering bundles of wood, he is charmed by her beauty. Returning home, he tells his father he would like to marry the girl. His father knows the poor farmer who is father of the girl and finds him honorable though poor. "What do you have to offer her? You have no trade," says the father. Kamalo replies, "But I am the son of a chief." A messenger is sent asking the girl, Chinowana, to marry Kamalo, but she refuses, saying, "Chiefs can be deposed. How will he care for a wife and children if this happens?" Kamalo becomes apprentice to a rug maker and soon is adept at his trade. He marries Chinowana. For a time they live happily until a neighboring tribe surprisingly attacks the village, capturing Kamalo and other young men. When they are placed in a cave, Kamalo asks for some string and weaves a small rug that is sent to the king for ransom. Recognizing Kamalo's handiwork, the chief pays the ransom, and the men are freed. Find this story in Eleanor B. Heady. *When the Stones Were Soft: East African Fireside Tales*, illus. Tom Feelings (New York: Knopf, 1985).

RUMPLESTILTSKIN: CLASSIC FOLKTALE

From Grimm's *Household Tales*, the greatest fun of this familiar story comes at the end when the princess discovers the name of the man who holds her captive. She toys with the little man, pretending not to know his name. On the third guess, the last she is allowed, she shouts, "Is your name Rumplestiltskin?" In spite of films and other media, the tale still works when told well. Find this story in Edna Johnson, Evelyn R. Sickels, Frances Clarke Sayers, and Carolyn Horovitz. *Anthology of Children's Literature*, 5th ed. (Boston: Houghton Mifflin, 1977).

THE SANDAL SELLER: NEW YEAR'S EVE, JAPANESE, CULTURAL

A poignant story is told about an old couple too poor to celebrate the New Year. They had no rice to make the traditional "moichi" cakes. New Year's Eve was not New Year's Eve without moichi. The old man took straw sandals he had made into town to sell. No one was interested in purchasing sandals, for they were busy preparing for the New Year. The sandal seller met a man selling charcoal who was also having bad luck. Neither sold their wares. In the end the two men agreed to trade, each taking the other's wares. The sandal seller arrived home very cold and tired, and the poor man laid the charcoal by the fire. Similar to the story of the "Shoemaker and the Elves," an elf appeared who looked exactly like the charcoal seller. The charcoal seller had given the old man magic charcoal, which the elf turned into gold and then disappeared. Find this story in Florence Sakade. *Urashima Taro and Other Japanese Children's Stories* (Rutland, VT: Charles E. Tuttle, 1959).

THE SLEEPING BEAUTY: CLASSIC FOLKTALE

This classic will be found in many Grimm story collections as "Little Briar Rose." Almost everyone is familiar with the princess who pricks her finger, placing herself and all around her in a long sleep. They are all awakened when a prince kisses the beautiful sleeping princess. Find this story in collections of Grimm's tales. See Edna Johnson, Evelyn R. Sickels, Frances Clarke Sayers, and Carolyn Horovitz. *Anthology of Children's Literature*, 5th ed. (Boston: Houghton Mifflin, 1977).

THE STORY OF THE THREE LITTLE PIGS: ANIMAL TALE

There are several versions of this classic tale. Children do not seem to be disturbed by the fact that the first two pigs do not survive. They seem satisfied that the third pig outwits the old wolf. Probably the use of repetitive phrases brings relief. Usually children follow the storyteller as the words are repeated, "I'll huff and I'll puff, and I'll blow your house down" and "By the hair of my chinny, chin, chin." A modern version is Steven Kellogg. *The Three Little Pigs* (New York: HarperCollins, 2002). See also Edna Johnson, Evelyn R. Sickels, Frances Clarke Sayers, and Carolyn Horovitz. *Anthology of Children's Literature*, 5th ed. (Boston: Houghton Mifflin, 1977).

TALK: AFRICAN TALE, HUMOR

"Talk" is one of my favorite African cumulative tales. It follows the farmer, the fisherman, and the weaver who hear animals or inanimate objects speak to them, including a yam. Together, they run to report these incidences to the chief. The chief refuses to believe the stories, threatening to punish the three for disturbing the peace. The chief is startled when he rises from his stool and the stool says, "Imagine a talking yam!" See Charlotte K. Brooks, ed. *African Rhythms: Selected Stories and Poems* (New York: Simon and Schuster, 1974).

THE TALKING POT: POOR VERSUS THE RICH

A poor man, down on his luck, had nothing but a wife, a house, and one lone cow. He took the cow to sell at market. On the way, he met a stranger who wanted to exchange a three-legged iron pot for the cow. The poor man was just about to refuse the bargain when the pot talked and said,

"Take me, take me, and you'll never be sorry." The man changed his mind and made the trade. When he arrived home with the pot, his wife was furious. The pot began to speak, "Clean me and shine me and put me on the fire." Stunned, the wife wondered what else the pot could do. "I will skip, I will skip," it said, and it did just that—skipped off to the rich man's house. Seeing such a beautiful shiny pot, the rich man's wife decided to make in it a grand pudding. When the pudding was made, the pot ran, taking the pudding back to poor man. After several such trips, the rich man vowed to get even, but when he tried to grab the pot, he found he was stuck, and the pot ran away with him, all the way to the North Pole. Find this story in Mary C. Hatch. *13 Danish Tales* (New York: Harcourt: 1947).

TEENY TINY: A "JUMP" TALE

Young children in particular love the repetitious use of the words *teeny tiny* in every phrase, and children in all the early grades like to be a little bit frightened by the teeny tiny voice seeking to recover the teeny tiny bone that the teeny tiny woman found and placed in her cupboard. Find this story in Joseph Jacob. *English Fairy Tales* (New York: Putnam, 1892), and many other collections.

TEN SUNS: CHINESE LEGEND, CULTURAL

This Chinese legend is about De Jun, his wife Xi He, and their ten sons (suns). The suns gave light to and warmed the earth. Every day, one of the suns took turns crossing the sky. One day the boys got bored with the slow routine of waiting their turn with nothing else to do. They disobeyed their parents and traveled in a group, warming up the earth to the point that everything was dying and earth people were afraid for the survival of the earth. When the father learned of this, he handled the matter and turned the boys into crows as punishment. (This sounds a little like global warming.) A picture book version of this tale with colorful illustrations by Yongsheng Xuan states on the cover that this is one of the oldest legends of China, dating back to the Shang dynasty of 1523 BC to 1027. Eric A. Kimmel. *Ten Suns: A Chinese Legend* (New York: Holiday House, 1998).

THE THREE SILLIES: HUMOR

This droll tale is so silly that it seems only appropriate for the young, although adult audiences have been known to chuckle during some scenes. The protagonist sets out to find three sillies who are sillier than the woman he had promised to marry. Only then would he return and be wed. He finds three sillies, including one man who has never learned how to put on his pants. The protagonist observes as the man hangs up his pants and attempts to jump into them! Find this story in Joseph Jacob. *English Fairy Tales* (New York: Putnam, 1948).

THE THREE STRONG WOMEN: EQUALITY OF WOMEN, JAPANESE, CULTURAL

In a tale from Japan, three women are able to defeat the famed wrestler Forever-Mountain. The conceited male wrestler learns his lesson when he meets the three women. After being trained by the females, Forever-Mountain returns to wrestling, defeats every contestant, and wins prize money. Content with his winnings, the wrestler becomes a farmer and marries the youngest of the three women. See Claus Stamn. *Three Strong Women*, illus. Kazue Mizumura (New York: Viking, 1962).

THE TIME JACK SOLVED THE HARDEST RIDDLE: HUMOR, APPALACHIAN

Audiences love riddle tales, and this one is especially charming. It provides an invitation for audience participation if the storyteller wishes. Several riddles are disclosed, and at each disclosure, audiences like to guess. The storyteller will need skill in maintaining control and continuing the tale. At the time, Jack is a grown man, still exploring and looking for things he has not seen before. He saves a young girl from the bottom of a well and finds out she is the dead king's daughter, hated and placed in the well to die by the queen. The two decide to travel together, but when they secretly return to the king's house for the girl's traveling clothes, the queen foils their plans. The queen offers to save the girl's life but only if Jack marries her instead of the princess. After a series of events, Jack learns that the queen loves riddles and offers to have a riddle contest. If she's the winner, he will marry her, and if Jack's the winner, the girl who has been sent again to the well will be saved. The contest begins, and Jack can't find a way to win. The queen offers Jack a one-year reprieve to solve the final riddle, "If a woman should want to spend her life with only one man, what would she desire in that man?" The story moves on, and Jack, receiving help from an old woman, solves the riddle. Find this story in Donald Davis. *Southern Jack Tales* (Atlanta, GA: August House, 1992).

THE TIME JACK TOLD A BIG TALE: HUMOR, APPALACHIAN

In this story, Jack himself is a storyteller. The king, being old and infirm, was bored and worried about his daughter's future. He wanted to pick a husband for her before he died. He decided to rid himself of boredom and at the same time choose a husband for his daughter. He would have all the men who wished to marry his daughter come and tell him stories, and the one who could make him say, "That's not true!" would be the chosen one. One day Jack's brothers encouraged him to have a try. Audiences giggle when they hear the description of Jack's attire for the visit—an overcoat his daddy used to wear that reached to the ground, a hat that came down over his ears, and a mowing scythe hanging on his side as a substitute for a sword. It is a story about a flea, similar to the Spanish story titled "The Flea," that makes the king say the winning words. This story is from Donald Davis. *Southern Jack Tales* (Atlanta, GA: August House, 1992).

THE TINKER AND THE GHOST: GHOST TALE

For years no one had lived in the haunted castle, where voices moaned and from which wails could be heard. On Halloween, flaring lights appeared from the chimney! Then came a brave tinker named Esteban, who claimed to fear nothing. He agreed to sleep in the castle. If he could banish the ghost, he would receive much money. He asked for some wood, a side of bacon, a flask of wine, a dozen fresh eggs, and a frying pan. Loaded with all these things, he entered the castle, built a fire, and began to cook the bacon and eggs. He heard a voice from the chimney say, "Oh, me! Oh, me!" Later it said, "Look out below! I'm falling!" Esteban answered, "Just don't fall into the frying pan." In seconds, down the chimney fell a man's leg clothed in half a pair of trousers. Subsequently, the voice continued to call, "Look out below! I'm falling," and Esteban, unperturbed, asked it not to fall in his food. He ate and drank his wine while more body parts fell, including the head. The man-ghost said, "You are the only one who has stayed here until I could get myself together." It was not over; the man explained that he had stolen money that was hidden where he buried it by the tree outside. If Esteban would help him, his soul could go to heaven. There were three bags: one of copper to be given to the church, one of silver to be given to the poor, and the bag of gold Esteban could keep. They retrieved the money, with Esteban's agreement to carry out the ghost's wishes. The ghost disappeared. The next morning, the townspeople came to carry away Esteban's body as they had done with past visitors. Esteban was alive and collected his money from the owner of the castle, gathered his bags of coins, and took care of his promises. With his riches, Esteban lived a pleasant, idle life.

This Spanish folktale can be found in Edna Johnson, Evelyn R. Sickels, Frances Clarke Sayers, and Carolyn Horovitz. *Anthology of Children's Literature*, 5th ed. (New York: Houghton Mifflin, 1977). It is credited to "Three Golden Oranges" by Ralph Steele Boggs and Mary Gould Davis.

THE TORTOISE AND THE HARE: AESOP'S FABLE

Tortoise appears frequently in collections of stories from various parts of Africa. Like the real animal, tortoise is physically slow but smart. He lives a long life and becomes wise by studying the lives and problems of other animals. In some stories he is punished for trickery, as in "The King and the Magic Drum." The Aesop's fable of the overconfident Rabbit in a race with Tortoise has lasting charm. Find this story in Janet Stevens. *The Tortoise and the Hare: An Aesop Fable* (New York: Holiday House, 1984).

TORTOISE AND THE MAGIC DRUM: AFRICAN TALE, CULTURAL

This story is found under several titles including, "The King and the Magic Drum." Set in Nigeria, a king owns a magic drum. When he beats the drum, a marvelous array of foods appears, making a feast for all in the locale. When enemies threaten, their hostility subsides with the appearance of such wonderful fare. However, there is a secret to the drum's magic. Anyone who owns and uses it must never step on a twig. In the version starring the tortoise, he is in a palm tree cutting down nuts for his family, and one of the nuts falls on the ground. He sees one of the king's wives with her child retrieve the palm nut, which the child eats. Tortoise calls the wife a thief and complains to the king. The king listens to his wife's story but feels he has to repay Tortoise, somehow. Tortoise demands the magic drum. The king gives it to him but does not tell him the secret. At first, Tortoise is very pleased with the drum's magic and has feasts for the villagers just as the king did. But one day he trips on a twig, and the magic disappears. Enemies appear and drive Tortoise from the village to hide in the mud near the riverbank. There he and his family can be found living today.

A much longer version of the story is "The King and the Magic Drum." This one is basically the same but contains many intricate and compelling changes and exploits, including the theft of the drum by Tortoise's own son. See Thomas A. Nevin. *The King's Magic Drum: A Yoruba Folk Tale*, illus. Ian Lusted (Durbanville, South Africa: Garamond, 1996), or Elphinstone Dayrell. *Folk Stories from Southern Nigeria* at http://www.sacred-texts.com/afr/fssn/index.htm.

TWINS: BROTHERS, AFRICAN TALE, CULTURAL

For those who wish to try a long tales, this one has mysticism, beasts, love, intrigue, and tragedy. In Yoruba land, a man and his wife had many children who all died young. Instructed by the priest, they were willing to give away all their worldly goods to have two healthy twins. They made the sacrifice and survived with the help of family and friends. Twins Taiwo and Kehinde were born. The boys grew up and left home, taking separate paths. Father gave them each one of twin leopards, twin hawks, twin cats, twin dogs, twin knives, and twin swords. When the boys separated, they each stuck a knife in a tree and promised to meet at that place in five years. Kehinde soon found a town where he settled and studied medicine. Taiwo traveled farther, coming to a place by the sea controlled by Olokun the sea monster. The king's daughter was being sacrificed to appease Olokun so he would not be angry and cover the land with water. Taiwo released the daughter, fought and killed the six-headed monster, and continued on his way. A dishonest general claimed to have accomplished the feat and was promised the chief's beautiful daughter in marriage. The girl told the story of being saved by Taiwo, but no one believed her. Preparation was made for the daughter's marriage to the general. Upon the death of the chief, the general would become king. Events followed that lead to Taiwo's proof that he was the brave warrior who killed the monster. The general was punished, and Taiwo married the princess. But all was not well, for when it was time for the brothers to meet at the tree, Kehinde found that Taiwo had been turned to stone by the old mother of the sea monster. Being a doctor, Kehinde knew how to protect himself from her. He killed the monster's mother, entered her compound, and using the woman's magic fluids revived Taiwo. Together they returned to seek their parents and found that both were now dead. Monuments were erected with more magic. Kehinde returned to practice medicine but did not live very long. Taiwo spent many years as king and had many children. When he died, the twin animals also died, but his son became the first king of Oyo. This story is found in Abayomi Fuja. *Fourteen Hundred Cowries and Other African Tales*, illus. Abayomi Fuja (New York: Washington Square, 1973).

WHY MOSQUITOES BUZZ IN PEOPLE'S EARS: AFRICAN POURQUOI TALE

Mosquito tells lizard that he saw a farmer digging yams as big as mosquitoes, which is a lie. Lizard (iguana) is so upset that he puts sticks in his ears, frightening Python. Python scares Rabbit, Rabbit scares Crow, and Crow alarms Monkey, who reacts and an owlet is killed. Owl is too sad to wake the sun, so King Lion calls a meeting to determine who caused this disaster. The chain of events leads back to Mosquito, who hides to escape punishment. Since that time mosquitoes buzz in people's ears to determine whether they are still angry. The picture book version of this story by Verna Aardema, illustrated by Diane and Leo Dillon, won the Caldecott Award in 1976. See Verna Aardema. *Why Mosquitoes Buzz in People's Ears*, illus. Diane and Leo Dillon (New York: Dial, 1975, 1992).

WHY THE HYRAX HAS NO TAIL: AFRICAN POURQUOI TALE

To be added to a repertoire of pourquoi tales, many having the same general theme, is the hyrax who was too lazy to go and get his tail when called. The same version appears representing other animals without tails. Find this story in Susan Feldmann. *African Myths and Legends* (New York: Dell, 1963).

ELEVEN

Three Original Stories

There is always the possibility of creating your own story. After learning the pattern of folktales, personal stories can be formatted with group appeal. After years of telling other people's stories, it is not unusual for storytellers to test their creative prowess.

Personal Note: I have told original stories. While I was singing with the Gwen Wyatt Chorale in 2001, the Dalai Lama initiated a World Festival of Sacred Music designed to help nations realize that we can all use music as a way to connect with each other. Churches and other organizations all over Los Angeles participated in the celebration. When the chorale performed, I was asked to present a story at the intermission of our choir's musical offering. Feeling the need for making my own personal contribution to this worthy program, I wrote a story, which follows. Later I printed copies and gave most of them away, although some were purchased. A copy is in the Los Angeles County Public Library collection.

CHIAFRA, CHILD OF AFRICA

High on a hill in the Great Smoky Mountains, there lived a man and wife of African descent. They called themselves Wolf and Walini in honor of the First Nations tribe with whom they lived for many years. While living as slaves, together they had jumped the broom, and their union had produced four children. Cruelly, every child was lost to the horrors of slavery. When the last child died, Wolf and Walini, then called John and Sarah, began to plot their escape.

Instead of following the river north like many, they made their way northwest to the mountains of North Carolina bordering Tennessee. Sick and exhausted, they were found by hunters from one of America's tribal nations. Some members of that tribe had themselves narrowly escaped slavery. Treated by the medicine man, John and Sarah regained their health and were given the names Wolf and Walini. They lived as part of the tribe until laws were passed demanding that First Nation tribes return all escaped slaves. The chief discussed the matter with Wolf and Walini and allowed them to leave. On the day of departure, the chief gave Wolf a large drum that when filled with water made a great sound.

"Find a place to hide high in the hills. When the clouds gather around the mountains like smoke and the thunder speaks, listen for our drums," said the chief to Wolf. "This is the way we will speak to you. When your drum answers, we will know that all is well with Wolf and Walini."

In a not-too-distant wooded area at the top of a hill, Wolf and Walini found a deserted cabin. Here, they felt they could be safe. Having learned much from their tribal family, the pair survived by eating berries, nuts, vegetables, and game from the nearby woods. Because the woods were dense with no paths, Wolf and Walini developed a signal, a call that would help lead one to the other. If one was out of sight of the other or was late arriving at their small hill home, the call could be heard echoing through the hills:

> Oh ye, oh yei ye ye!
> Oh ye, oh yei ye ye!

When storms rolled over the Great Smoky Mountains, the sound of drums could be heard in the distance. Between the crashes of thunder, the answer from Wolf and Walini signaled "All is well."

As time passed, Wolf and Walini became familiar with the woods surrounding their home. They soon began to gather more fruits and nuts than they could eat. The two of them decided to venture out into a village that they had discovered nearby.

At first, they were fearful, and Walini kept watch while Wolf sold fruits and nuts at the village store. With the money they earned, they bought small items for their home. Finding no notices posted for runaway slaves in the village, they felt it was safe to return.

During one visit, Wolf and Walini saw a little girl, dirty and uncared for, outside of the village store. Walini walked over and spoke to the young girl, "Hello. What is your name?" The child's eyes lit up as she smiled but said nothing. While selling their nuts and berries, Walini asked the storekeeper about the young girl. He answered, "She can hear, but she don't speak. She don't belong to nobody 'round here. I don't know where she sleeps, but she's always going roun' place to place begging for food. I don't let her come in here!"

When Wolf and Walini left the store, the child was still there. Walini, lonely for children, told her husband, "We should take this child home with us." Wolf agreed, and Walini took the little girl by the hand and led her through the woods and up the path to their home.

Inside the cabin the child walked around examining everything, including baskets that Walini had woven. "What will we call her?" Walini asked Wolf.

"Look at her. She is surely a child of Africa. Her skin is smooth and dark like the darkest pecans, and her hair coils close to her head. She has eyes of great beauty that slant upward at the corners. We will call her Chiafra. She will be our child of Africa," Wolf answered.

The new parents taught Chiafra all they knew about counting and reading. Walini taught her to weave baskets in the style of the First Nations joined with patterns from African memories. Chiafra's small hands with long slender fingers were suited to this task.

Soon Chiafra wove beautiful baskets with her own designs. The baskets were so beautiful that there was a great demand for them. The little family began to prosper.

Since Chiafra had become a part of their family, Wolf and Walini seldom left the house without her. One very hot summer day, there were many goods to take to market. Walini said to Wolf, "I think it is too hot for the child to take that long trek through the woods. I believe it would be safe to leave her here. No one ever comes to this place, and we have been careful not to be followed home." Reluctantly, Wolf agreed.

"We will return as soon as possible," Walini told Chiafra. "If you get lonely, weave a basket, but don't leave the house. You could get lost in these woods." Chiafa nodded yes. Wolf and Walini went on their way.

Chiafra made herself content looking out of the window, chewing nuts and berries, and basket weaving. Later, she noticed that it was getting dark outside. She ran to the window and saw the darkest of clouds gathering around the mountains. "Wolf will not be here to send his message," she thought. On the occasion of past storms, Chiafra had become familiar with the ritual of drums.

As time passed and it became darker, Chiafra began to feel anxious. She stared out of the window as the storm began. "They should have been home by now," she thought. "I wonder what happened." As more time passed and her new parents had not returned, Chiafra began to cry. "What can I do?" she thought. "What can I do?"

Suddenly this child of Africa knew what she had to do. She ran to the cabin door and opened it to the wind and rain. Standing on the hill, she cupped her hands over her mouth and tried to make the sounds she had heard Wolf and Walini make. At first there was no sound, but soon a small voice emerged.

> Oh ye, oh yei ye ye!
> Oh ye, oh yei ye ye!

And then louder

OH YE, OH YEI YE YE!

OH YE, OH YEI YE YE!

Chiafra had found her voice. She called several times, and in the distance, she could hear the answer from Wolf and Walini. In the darkness and rain, they had tried to take a new route through the woods and had become lost. Chiafra's yells led them home.

Till this day, high on a certain hill in the Great Smoky Mountains, when the clouds gather like smoke and the thunder speaks, faint sounds of drums can be heard. The wind calls softly through the trees.

> Oooh ye, oooh yei yei yei
> Oooh ye, oooh yei yei yei.

The following story is a tall tale written in frustration after not being able to find a story about the African American tradition of eating black-eyed peas for good luck on New Year's Eve night and New Year's Day. Once I had heard that some African tribes saw the eye of the pea as the eye of God and used the peas in religious celebrations, but I have been unable to verify this.

LEGEND OF THE BLACK-EYED PEAS; OR STRONGER THAN A MULE

Jim was an ex-slave. For years he had saved money in a jar, hoping to buy his freedom, and then word came that all slaves were free. Jim took his jar of money and his few other possessions and set out on foot on the roads of eastern North Carolina. Somewhere around Winterville, he saw a sign that read "Small Plot of Land for Sale Cheap." Jim had just enough money to buy that plot and the shack that stood on it. It wasn't much, but it was his, and he was free. Jim did what he could to make the little shack livable. He bought some biddies and started to raise some chickens, and he planted a garden.

Nearby a man everyone called Old Thompson owned hundreds of acres of farmland. Jim went to him asking for work.

"You can work like the other sharecroppers," Old Thompson said. "When the crops come in, you get your share."

"How much?" asked Jim.

"Don't know now. Depends on how hard you work!" said Thompson.

Jim worked hard tilling, planting, tending, and harvesting the hundreds of acres of corn with the other sharecroppers and farmhands. At the end of the harvest, Old Thompson came to Jim's shack carrying a large sack.

"Here's your pay," he said to Jim. "Ain't much, but I had to buy all the seeds and the fertilizer and the equipment, so time you subtract for all that, don't leave much. But here, I brought you this sack of black-eyed peas. Jim shook his head and took the money and the peas. Every year it was the same thing: no money much and a sack of black-eyed peas. Jim dug a dry cellar to store those peas because they were filling up his little shack.

One year there came a drought, the worst they had ever seen in eastern North Carolina. There was no water to raise crops, and everyone in the area fell on hard times. For a while, Thompson did alright, being the richest man for miles around. But soon, you could see by his land and animals that the drought had taken its toll.

Meantime, because Jim had dug himself a deep well, he still had just enough water for himself and his few animals. To survive, he brought out those peas, a bag at the time, boiled them, and ate them. He pounded them into flour and fed them to his chickens and made hoe cakes. He managed to stay strong.

When the rains came, here comes Old Thompson, saying, "Now there's still time to raise some corn. If you work hard, I'll give you a share of the corn to sell at market." Jim agreed, and they raised some corn in time for harvest sales at the local market. Thompson brought Jim a small amount to sell. Jim hitched his old mule to his wagon and took that small portion to market. He sold the corn and was standing there talking to a friend, when he looked up the road and there came Old Thompson with his wagon piled high with corn. Now Thompson's mules weren't in such good shape because they hadn't been fed well during the drought and that was a might heavy load. Those mules were wheezing and snorting, and Old Thompson was whipping them so hard. Jim couldn't stand it. He ran out to the wagon and said to Thompson, "Ain't no need of whipping those mules to death!" To everyone's surprise, Jim unhitched the mules and pulled that wagon all by himself those last few feet to the market. Old Thompson shouted to all those standing by, "Look at that fool! He's stronger than a mule!"

Breathing hard, Jim turned to say, "No suh, ain't nothing but a man. I ain't nothing but a man!"

They tell me that soon after that Old Thompson got sick and died, but Jim prospered and became one of the largest land owners in that section of eastern North Carolina. Stories are still told about his strength and kindness. Since that time, African Americans have believed that black-eyed peas bring good luck. Every year on the night of New Year's Eve and on New Year's Day, many African American families eat black-eyed peas for good luck.

In 1978, I made a trip to my home in North Carolina, spending a week or more visiting and interviewing family and other African American people in their seventies to one hundred. My purpose was to learn from their anecdotes information and actual stories and to write some stories of my own from what I heard. From this came several stories that I have told.

Some were written down and printed. Knowing that children in many of the neighborhoods I served had no books, I printed some of these stories and gave them away at storytelling sessions. One title called "Carrie's Dream" is in both the Los Angeles City and Los Angeles County Public Library collections. It was translated into a play for children and presented at the National Theatre in Washington, DC.

The following story was told to me by a woman whose age was one hundred that year or the year before. She had been a country schoolteacher most of her life. This is my version of the story she told when I asked her about her siblings.

HAMBONE

Sing: Hambone, hambone where you been? Down to the grave and back again.

Georgia lived with her mama and papa on a large farm outside of the town of Greenville. She was six years old and loved attending the one-room schoolhouse several miles down the road. Georgia was an only child. At school she played with children from other distant farms. Her best friend at school lived many miles away and could not visit often. It was lonely at home. Every day, Georgia wished for a baby sister to keep her company.

Georgia asked her mother, "When am I going to have a brother or sister to play with me?

"When the time is right. Keep on wishing," Mama answered.

From that time on, Georgia asked her mother, "Is the time right for me to have a baby sister?"

To her surprise, one day Mama answered, "In nine months, but don't be surprised if it's a baby boy."

For nine months Georgia wished for a baby sister, and when the child was born, it was a girl. They named her Sally.

Georgia called the child "Baby Sister." She watched Sally, tickled her toes, and helped Mama change her diapers.

When Sally was big enough to walk, Georgia took her along everywhere she went—to gather eggs from the hens, to help pick beans, and to feed the hogs. Georgia was no longer lonely for company.

At dinner, Georgia sat next to Baby Sister, whose favorite food was ham. Mama said the child was "marked" because, while she had carried the child for nine months, she craved and ate lots of ham.

After Sally began to talk and there was ham for dinner, she would bounce up and down and sing, "Hambone, hambone, hambone."

Mama cut deep into the ham to find a piece of bone for sister to chew on quietly.

Georgia loved Baby Sister more than anything in the world.

One day Baby Sister got sick with the fever. Mama, Father, and Georgia worried.

There was no doctor to treat the baby, but Mama brought in an old lady who knew about healing. They treated Sally with every remedy they knew about, but Baby Sister did not survive.

She was buried at the edge of the farm in the family graveyard.

Georgia was so sad, she hardly ate. Mama and Papa tried to comfort their daughter and told her to start wishing again. But Georgia had no heart to make a wish. Sometimes when she sat on the porch of the farmhouse in the twilight, she was sure she could see Baby Sister standing at the gate, saying, "Hambone, hambone, hambone." Every time it happened, she told Mama.

Mama hugged Georgia and said, "Shhh, child. You still grieving. I know you miss your sister."

One evening, Mama, Father, and Georgia sat at the dinner table, ready to eat ham Mama cooked for dinner.

"I don't want to eat no ham!" Georgia cried.

Father said, "Georgia, you got to stop that nonsense! Baby Sister's gone, and you have to eat. Now take some of that ham."

There were slices of ham already cut off the bone, but Georgia picked up the big knife, and before anyone could stop her, she hacked off the end of that hambone, and the knife slipped, cutting off a small tip of her finger.

"Georgia! What are you doing?" yelled Mama. But before Mama could stop her, Georgia picked up that piece of hambone and the piece of her own finger and ran out to the edge of the farm. She dug with her hands, burying that bone and a little piece of herself in the dirt. Mama and Father had followed her.

Georgia said to them, "Now she has her hambone."

Sing: Hambone, hambone where you been? Down to the grave and back again.

TWELVE

Resources, Organizations, References

Storytelling organizations and festivals have emerged all over the United States and in other countries. Attending festivals and contacting organizations may be of great value for ideas and new stories and to view the enormous variety of tellers. Many listings are available from local libraries or on the Internet. Read and review the information carefully because many Internet listings are for or related to business organizations. For the past few years, storytelling has become a popular subject for businesses, focusing on the storytelling manner as a useful managerial and sales tool. Another important resource would be any cultural organizations in the community, particularly those dedicated to the arts.

Informational notes are added to most of the following selected examples of helpful resources.

THE AMERICAN FOLKLIFE CENTER

Cultural information about dances, dress, rituals, and more can be found at http://www.loc.gov/folklife.

AMERICAN LIBRARY ASSOCIATION, ETHNIC CAUCUSES AND OFFICE OF LIBRARY OUTREACH

The following ethnic organizations are affiliates of the American Library Association dedicated to providing the best and most creative services in communities where they are represented and in the world. Each of these groups can provide information about librarians who are expert storytellers. Many of them have studied stereotypical representations in story and lore that should be avoided.

- American Indian Library Association (AILA): Focuses on American Indians and Alaskan Natives. Their website is ailanet.org/author/aila.
- Asian/Pacific American Librarians Association (APALA): Represents diverse Asian and Pacific ancestries. Their website is www.apalaweb.org.
- Black Caucus of the American Library Association, Inc. (BCALA): Concerns itself with information services for African Americans and Africans in the Diaspora. Their website is www.bcala.org.
- Chinese American Librarians Association (CALA): Chinese librarians in collaboration with others "advance diversity and equality." Their website is CALA-web.org.
- REFORMA: The National Association to Promote Library and Information Services to Latinos and the Spanish Speaking: Promotes library service to the Spanish speaking. Their website is www.reforma.org.

Of special interest would be the AILA/APALA's Talk Story Project, BCALA's Reading Is Grand Program, and REFORMA's Noche de Cuentos Project.

Posted on the AILA site is the following:

> Talk Story: Sharing stories, sharing culture (www. talkstorytogether.org) is a literacy program that reaches out to Asian Pacific American (APA) and American Indian/Alaska Native (AIAN) children and their families. The program celebrates and explores their stories through books, oral traditions, and art to provide an interactive, enriching experience. 2013 will be the fourth year that AILA and APALA have partnered on the Talk Story project and allocated grant funding to libraries to implement programs geared towards the APA/AIAN communities.

The project has produced very helpful information including a list of picture books. Many of the titles listed are folk stories appropriate for telling. See talkstorytogether.org/american-indian-alaskan-native-book-list/picture-books

The Reading Is Grand Program celebrates families and encourages them to tell their stories: "Sharing stories, both oral and written are the building blocks of literacy." Dr. Claudette S. McLinn, cochair, is the contact person for this project. See www.bcalareadingisgrand.weebly.com

Noche de Cuentos: Celebrating the Power of Storytelling to Unite Communities is designed "to promote and preserve the art of storytelling within our Latino communities in the U.S." REFORMA partners with libraries in implementing story events. See http://nochedecuentos.org.

BLACK STORYTELLERS ALLIANCE

From their website, Black Storytellers Alliance is "story telling brought to life by Authentic Master Story Tellers . . . dedicated to assisting you in finding the information that you need about the power of the oral tradition as practiced by African people in the Diaspora. Our mission is to maintain the *art* of storytelling as a primary source for positive instruction and reinforcement of the rich beauty embodied in the telling of 'the story'!" See www.blackstorytellers.com.

INTERNATIONAL STORYTELLING CENTER

The center, located in Jonesborough, Tennessee, is sponsored by NSN. It includes varieties of storytelling materials and has a storytelling hall and gift shop. Their website is www.storytellingcenter.net/experience/visit-the-center.

NATIONAL ASSOCIATION OF BLACK STORYTELLERS

Based in Minnesota, the organization holds a national festival. In 2012 the title was "Signifyin' and Testifyin'."

THE NATIONAL STORYTELLERS LEAGUE (NSL)

Probably the oldest storytelling organization in United States, this group publishes *Story Art*, a quarterly periodical. Professional workshops, festivals, and conferences assist members and interested storytellers. Contact Jane Hill, National Treasurer, at 1219 W. Sanford St., Arlington, TX 76012. Their website is www.nslstorytellers.org.

NATIONAL STORYTELLING NETWORK (NSN)

With contact listed at Box 309, Jonesborough, Tennessee 37659, NSN has dues-paying members from all over the United States and some foreign countries. Programs are presented for storytellers, teachers, and librarians. The organization publishes *Storytelling Magazine*, catalogs, and directories and holds conventions. Their festivals are well known, especially the National Storytelling Festival held every October in Jonesborough. Their website is www.storynet.org.

STORY CORPS' GRIOT INITIATIVE

Story Corps Griot Initiative ensures that the voices, experiences, and life sources of African Americans will be preserved and presented with dignity. (*Griot* is pronounced "gree-oh.") Their website is storycorps.org/initiative/griot.

STORYTELL DISCUSSION LIST

Sponsored by the National Storytelling Network, this is an e-mail list of more than 500 subscribers worldwide for discussions about storytelling. www.storynet.org/storytell.html.

WORLD STORYTELLING DAY

World Storytelling Day is a global celebration of the art of storytelling celebrated at the spring equinox in the northern hemisphere and on the autumn equinox in the southern. On that day, people tell and listen to stories in many places and in many languages. The roots of this special day lie in the Swedish National Day of Storytelling held on March 20 each year. The Swedish effort to support storytellers was soon adopted by others. In 2009, World Storytelling Days were held in Europe, Asia, North America, South America, and Australia. In Mexico and South America, March 20 was already celebrated as the National Day of Storytellers. A coordinating theme is now designated for each year. In 2013, the theme was "Fortune and Fame," and in 2014, it will be "Monsters and Dragons." Several sites are available with more information, including www.storytellingday.net/detailed-information-world.html.

WORDCRAFT CIRCLE OF NATIVE WRITERS AND STORYTELLERS

A circle of native writers and storytellers formed Wordcraft to ensure the voices of native writers are heard. See http://www.wordcraftcircle.org.

YES! ALLIANCE: YOUTH, EDUCATORS, AND STORYTELLERS ALLIANCE

The group proclaims their goal is "to inspire and nurture storytelling by and for youth. Members include youth storytelling coaches, teachers, teaching artists, librarians, full-time storytellers, and other mentors who view storytelling as a vital essential art, as well as student storytellers who want to learn more about the art and craft of the oral tradition." See yesalliance.org.

REFERENCE MATERIALS AND STORY COLLECTIONS

A former president of the American Folklore Society acknowledges the complexity of the African continent and the enormous variety of cultural approaches to "story making." In the introduction to this collection, he states, "Stories operate like proverbs, as a means of depersonalizing, of universalizing by couching the description of how specific people are acting in terms of how people have always acted" (p. 2). There are some stories, such as "Why the Hare Runs Away," that can be told to children, but many of the stories are more appropriate for adults. Those in the section titled "Stories to Discuss and Even Argue About" are obviously designed for discussion. Each ends with a dilemma. One example is "An Eye for an Eye," in which a poor, young man is favored by and marries the king's daughter. After the king dies, she offers him the chance to bring his father to live in the compound nearby and to marry her widowed mother. When the father and her mother get in a fight, he knocks the mother's eye out. The girl demands that her husband do the same to his father or leave. Leaving would cause the husband to be as destitute as he was when they first met. What should he do?

Abrahams, Roger. *African Folktales: Traditional Stories of the Black World* (New York: Pantheon Books, 1983).

Alegria, Ricardo, ed., and Elizabeth Culburt, trans. *The Three Wishes: A Collection of Puerto Rican Folk Tales*. Illus. Lerenzo Homan (New York: Harcourt, 1969).
    Contains twenty-three of the most popular Puerto Rican tales told by Alegria and skillfully translated. The title story will be a familiar theme to many: A woodsman's wife is kind to an old man, who grants her three wishes. She uses the first, wishing her husband was there. He appears and hearing the story is angry that she used one of the wishes, which could have brought great wealth. In anger, he wishes that she would grow ears like a donkey. In remorse, he wishes for the happiness they had before. Pleased at that realization of happiness being better than wealth, the old man grants them one last favor, a child.

Anderson, Graham. *Fairytale in the Ancient World* (London: Routledge, 2000).
    Admitting the difficulty in defining *fairy tale*, this author asks whether the fairy tale of today existed in the ancient world. His definition of *fairy tale* is "short, imaginative, traditional tales with a high moral context." Anderson studies the characteristics of common tales, such as "Snow White" and "Little Red Riding Hood," from unusual and ancient sources, including ancient Jewish and Sumerian stories. He discusses who would have told the stories and why.

Asian Cultural Center of UNESCO. *Folk Tales from Asia for Children Everywhere*, books 1–6 (New York: Weatherhill, 1977).
   Folktales from Asia delightfully presented for children.

Baker, Augusta. *The Golden Lynx and Other Tales*. Illus. Johannes Troyer (New York: Lippincott, 1960).
   A collection of sixteen fairy tales from Norway, Demark, Sweden, and India, now out of print but available in large libraries.

Bauman, Stephanie G., ed. *Storytime for Children* (Santa Barbara, CA: Libraries Unlimited, 2011).
   Includes suggested storytelling patterns for groups of children ages zero to twelve. Patterns for multicultural festivals, such as Hanukkah and Diwali (Festival of Lights), could be very useful for teachers.

Belpré, Pura. *The Tiger and the Rabbit and Other Tales*. Illus. Tomie de Paola (New York: Lippincott, 1965).
   Eighteen Puerto Rican tales are told by this writer and storyteller.

Bierhost, John, ed. *Latin American Folktales: Stories from Hispanic and Indian Traditions* (New York: Pantheon, 2000).
   One hundred fifteen stories from various parts of Latin America are recorded here. The narratives are both ancient and modern. Some are based in religion. Many of the stories are geared toward older youth and adults.

Birch, Carolyn. *The Whole Story Handbook: Using Imagery to Complete the Story Experience* (Atlanta, GA: August House, 2000).
   Provided is a detailed look at imagery and how to effectively use it in storytelling. Among her writings, Birch coauthored with Melissa Heckler a recommended essay titled "Building Bridges with Stories" in David Leeming and Marion Sader's *Storytelling Encyclopedia* (Phoenix, AZ: Oryx, 1997).

Blayer, Irene, and Mark Cronlund Anderson. *American Narratives and Cultural Identity: Selected Readings* (New York: Peter Lang, 2004).
   Includes among other essays and articles, Maria F. Valdez's "Storytelling and Cultural Identity in Latin America," pp. 9–27.

Boyd, Brian. *On the Origin of Stories: Evolution, Cognition, and Fiction* (Cambridge, MA: Harvard University Press, 2009).
   This author examines why we tell stories and why our minds are adept at or shaped to understand stories.

Brody, Ed, Jay Godspinner, Katie Green, Rosa Leventhal, and Joe Percino, eds. *Spinning Tales, Weaving Hope: Stories, Storytelling and Activities for Peace, Justice and the Environment*, 2nd ed. (Philadelphia: New Society, 2002).

Sponsored by the Stories for World Change Network, permission is given by the authors to tell their tales, which give messages of peace and justice. The writers, who spent many years in research, present activities, songs, and a bibliography of "tellable" tales from other sources.

Brooks, Charlotte K., ed. *African Rhythms, Selected Stories and Poems.* Photos by Walter Brooks (New York: Pocket Books, Simon and Shuster, 1978).

This book was not designed for children but for students and adults familiarizing themselves with bits and pieces of cultural information and lore. The introduction speaks of the book as a "collection of African writings—by Africans—whose intent is to reflect what Africa was and is." It does include some stories for telling, but most are for older audiences.

Campbell, Joseph. *Joseph Campbell and the Power of the Myth: Conversations with Bill Moyers* (PBS, 1987).

This series of conversations would be interesting for classes, discussion groups, and festival showings. Excerpts are offered for each in the series on the Internet at www.pbs.org.

Campoy, F. Isabel, and Alma Flor Ada. *Cuentos que Contaban Nuestras Abuelas: Cuentos Populares Hispanicos* [*Tales Our Abuelitas Told: A Hispanic Folktale Collection*] (New York: Atheneum, 2006).

Beautifully presented tales, some of which were actually told to the writers by their abuelitas, are included. Such tales as "The Little Horse of Seven Colors" from Mexico are popular. These stories, some short and others long, capture the emotions of Latinos around the world. Some have similar themes as familiar everyday tales but are special to a given culture.

Chapman, Abraham, ed. *Literature of the American Indians: Views and Interpretations: A Gathering of Indian Memories, Symbolic Contexts, and Literary Criticism* (New York: New America, 1975).

Fascinating legends are told at the beginning of this title, which also contains challenging essays about the handling of literature from tribal America. There is an essay by Vine Deloria and other commentaries. Included legends are told by George Copway, or Kah-Ge-Ga-Gah-Bowh (1818–1863). He was a chief of the Ojibway Nation. A story called "Legend Third, Thunder's Nest" is about the origins of thunder. The great sounds come from the wings of mighty birds of the past. With a blink of the bird's eyes, the lightning flashes.

Cole, Johanna, comp. *Best-Loved Folktales of the World.* Illus. Jill Karla Schwartz (New York: Doubleday, 1982).

More than two hundred folk and fairy tales are included from around the world. Stories are categorized by geographic regions, with descriptions of plots and characters. Included are the favorites of folklorists and writers representing East and West Europe, Asia, the Caribbean, America, and Africa.

Cook, Elizabeth. *The Ordinary and the Fabulous: An Introduction to Myths, Legends, and Fairy Tales*, 2nd ed. (Cambridge, UK: Cambridge University Press, 1976).

Observing the value in stories and storytellers, Cook presents European myths, medieval literature, and folklore and fairy tales for the classroom and use elsewhere. An annotated list of books is of value.

Crouch, Marcus. *The Whole World Storybook*. Illus. William Stobbs (Oxford: Oxford University Press, 1983).

Twenty-six tales from around the world are told with verve and energy.

Cullum, Carolyn N. *The Storytime Sourcebook: A Compendium of Ideas and Resources for Storytellers* (New York: Neal-Schuman, 1999).

Designed for librarians, teachers, and media specialists but especially good for teachers, many subjects with songs and crafts for the very young are included. Topical themes are used to help formulate programs. Included is a holiday calendar.

Davis, Donald. *Southern Jack Tales* (Little Rock, AR: August House, 1992).

The author is also a recognized storyteller who recounts the "Jack Tales" of his youth growing up in the Appalachian Mountains of North Carolina. He states in the foreword, "I remember having great pleasure in just hanging around my grandparents' front porch so that I could listen to the old people 'just talk'" (p. 25). The book contains thirteen entertaining stories of Jack and his fortunes.

De Almeida, Livia, Ana Portella, and Margaret Read McDonald, eds. *Brazilian Folktales* (Englewood, CO: Libraries Unlimited, 2006).

A rich brew of more than forty Brazilian tales can be savored here. There are humorous stories of the trickster and enchanting folklore. The background of the indigenous people is discussed. Stories also reflect African–Portuguese influences and mixtures of all cultures. Few collections are available with Brazilian themes. This is an important resource.

De Las Casas, Diane, foreword by Margaret Read McDonald. *The Story Biz Handbook: How to Manage Your Storytelling Career from the Desk to the Stage* (Westport, CT: Libraries Unlimited, 2008).

Contains details and resources for the professional storyteller, including many helpful websites.

De Spain, Pheasant. *The Emerald Lizard: Fifteen Latin American Folktales to Tell*. World Storytelling Series (Atlanta, GA: August House, 2005).

De Spain spent three decades exploring Latin American countries, customs, and cultures. In this volume are fifteen tales, including myths and legends of countries in Central and South America, enthusiastically told. The story of "Juan Bobo," who dresses as a pig in his mother's best clothing, is told here and in other sources.

East, Kathy, Rebecca L. Thomas, and Catherine Bart, series eds. *Across Cultures: A Guide to Multicultural Literature for Children* (Westport, CT: Libraries Unlimited, 2007).

Designed to encourage diversity, this title lists four hundred books of fiction and nonfiction for grades preschool to 6. There are many suggestions for integrating multicultural books and stories into the curriculum. The section on folktales from various places includes "Cinderella" stories from Mexico, the Caribbean, and more. There is also a section on pourquoi stories, some familiar and some unique.

Feldmann, Susan. *African Myths and Tales* (New York: Dell, Laurel Books, 1963).

One hundred eight myths and tales are included, edited, and introduced by Feldmann. Included are stories from a variety of tribes. Many have subject matter and a quality that will appeal to adults and young adults. There is a section with trickster tales, including "How Spider Obtained the Sky God's Stories," an Ashanti tale. Also included is "Why the Sun and Moon Live in the Sky," attributed to the Efik-Ibibio.

Floyd, E. Randall. *Ghost Lights: And Other Encounters with the Unknown* (Atlanta, GA: August House, 1993).

With a journalistic approach, Floyd writes about ghosts, monsters, miracles, and strange occurrences, including mysterious airships, Mark Twain's dream, and other baffling and bizarre tales that are the "stuff" of urban myths. His fare is of appeal to older youth, upper elementary through high school. Fifty-four bizarre tales of mysterious occurrences are included.

Floyd, Randall. *Ghost Stories from the American Southwest* (Atlanta, GA: August House, 1991).

One hundred forty-two ghost stories with notes are included from the region. Many are perfect for geography and history, classes such as one from the Okefenokee, "The Lost Maiden," or a tale about ghosts of the Alamo.

Floyd, Randall. *Great American Mysteries: Raining Snakes, Fabled Cities of Gold, Strange Disappearances, and Other Baffling Tales* (Atlanta, GA: August House, 1991).

Thirty-eight mysterious happenings in America become spooky, mysterious tales of enchantment in this title.

Forest, Heather. *Wisdom Tales from Around the World*, World Storytelling Series (Atlanta, GA: August House, 1996).

A collection of traditional tales from around the world reflecting the cumulative wisdom of Sufi, Zen, Taoist, Buddhist, Jewish, Christian, African, and Native American cultures. Fifty stories for ages ten to adult reveal various levels of cultural beliefs. An extensive bibliography and references are available for further study.

Fuja, Abayomi, collector. *Fourteen Hundred Cowries and Other African Tales.* Illus. Ademola Olugebefola (New York: Pocket Books, 1975).

With an introduction by Anne Pellowski, the book presents thirty-four Yoruba tales. Some are more appropriate for adult audiences, but others have general appeal.

Garrity, Linda. *The Tale Spinner: Folktales, Themes, and Activities.* Illus. Emelia Markovich (Golden, CO: Fulcrum, 1999).

Included are units for teachers on traditional folklore, and listed are many versions of tales from various cultures, such as "Cinderella," including a Vietnamese version. "The Traveling Musician" has Spanish words inserted" — *cabra vieja* (old goat), *perro viejo* (old dog), *gato viejo* (old cat), and *gallo viejo* (old rooster).

Gerson, Mary-Joan. *Fiesta Feminina: Celebrating Women in Mexican Folktales.* Illus. Maya Christina Gonzales (Cambridge, MA: Barefoot Books, 2005).

A collection of folktales focusing on the important role of women from various cultures in Mexico. The women are brave, clever, and powerful, as in "Rosha," about the girl who rescues the sun, or the "Story of the Moon," who prefers to remain unmarried. These are short but richly presented tales.

Goss, Linda, and Marian E. Barnes. *Talk That Talk: An Anthology of African American Storytelling* (New York: Simon and Schuster, 1989).

Stories from the United States, Africa, and the Caribbean are categorized as African American folklore, including family stories and moral tales.

Goss, Linda, and Clay Goss. *Jump Up and Say! A Collection of Black Storytelling* (New York: Simon and Schuster, 1995).

The volume includes stories, poems, and informational articles that individually and collectively explore the experiences of African Americans. Some articles and stories are written by Africans from the continent. Ossie Davis's introduction offers, "Here is a feast, a dazzling display of narrative art at its most personal and its most profound." Within the feast of praise songs, information about spirituals, personal stories, and ghost stories are Anansi and Br'er Rabbit stories, which are fun to tell.

Green, Jen. *Myths of China and Japan* (Austin, NY: Raintree, Steck, Vaugh, Harcourt, 2002).

In only forty-eight pages, with lush colorful photographs, creation stories from China and Japan are included for cultural or multicultural story programs. For example, the creation of Japan was by Izanagi and his wife Izanami. The brief historical and cultural introduction is informative and challenges further study. A glossary at the end and reading list/video websites are helpful.

Greene, Ellin, and Janice M. Del Negro. *Storytelling Art and Technique*, 4th ed. Foreword by Jack Zipes (Santa Barbara, CA: Libraries Unlimited, 2010).

Designed for librarians and media specialists, this title includes information about the history of storytelling in libraries, storytelling training, some important pioneers in the field, how to plan a storytelling workshop and ends with an exhaustive list of "Resources for the Storyteller."

Hale, Thomas. *Griots and Griottes: Master of Words and Music* (Bloomington: Indiana University Press, 2007).

An in-depth study of this uniquely African profession is discussed and examined extensively in this text. In an Internet article about his research titled "Keepers of the Flame," Hale writes about the empowerment of stories: "Women, children and men are empowered by the story." Speaking of West African women singing story songs, he believes much is learned about the women singing the songs: "These women are empowered in what appears to be a male-dominated society."

Hale, Thomas C. *Scribe, Griot and Novelist: Narrative Interpreters of the Songhay Empire Followed by the Epic of Askia Mohammed, Recounted by Nouhou malio* (Gainesville: University of Florida Press, 1990).

Hale centers his studies on the Songhai people, with stories of kings and rulers.

Hamilton, Martha, and Mitch Weiss. *Children Tell Stories: A Teaching Guide* (Katonah, NY: R. C. Owen, 1990).

Aimed at teachers of kindergarten to eighth grade, detailed directions are given for teaching storytelling to children. Extensive tips and samples for integrating stories into the curriculum are included. The book is useful for any adult leaders.

Hamilton, Virginia. *The People Could Fly: American Black Folktales*. Illus. Leo and Diane Dillon (New York: Knopf, 1985).

With an enlightening introduction, Hamilton presents animal tales; tales of the real, extravagant, and fanciful; tales of the supernatural; and slave tales of freedom. Included in the last section is the title story "The People Could Fly." There are endnotes after each tale, helpful to readers, teachers, and storytellers. A bibliography lists sources for other versions of the tales. This title is listed on the Internet at teachingbooks.net.

Hamilton, Virginia. *A Ring of Tricksters: Animal Tales from America, The West Indies and Africa* (New York: Blue Sky Press/Scholastic, 1997).

History and theories of the trickster are explained by Hamilton. Sources for information are included, and examples of "gullah" speech are explained.

Haven, Kendall, and Mary Gay Ducey. *Crash Course on Storytelling* (Westport, CT: Libraries Unlimited, 2007).

Although this title seems mostly designed for the librarian-storyteller, it includes useful definitions and information. Attributes of the storyteller are examined, and suggestions for successful telling are included.

Heady, Eleanor. *When Stone Were Soft: East African Fireside Tales* (New York: HarperCollins, 1968).

A sample of stories told in Kenya, Uganda, and Tanzania. A running story at the beginning of each tale connects them all.

Hernandez, Antonio. *The Eagle and the Rainbow: Timeless Tales from Mexico.* Illus. Tomie de Paola (New York: Golden, Fulcrum Kids, 1997).

Stories about the endurance runners and Aztec warriors of the tribes of Mexico are recorded. Each story is followed by a brief history of the tribe of origin.

Hirschfelder, Arlene, Paulette Fairbanks Molin (Minnesota Chippewa Tribe from White Earth Reservation), and Yvonne Wakin (Cherokee/Arab). *American Indian Stereotypes in the World of Children: A Reader and Bibliography* (Metuchen, NJ: Scarecrow, 1999).

Challenging articles on the use of American Indian symbolism, images, and ideas in media, sports logos, and more are informative and important for storytellers. Themes of essays include Thanksgiving, Pocahontas, and the military. The bibliography is extensive.

Hoke, Helen. *Dragons, Dragons, Dragons.* Pictures by Carol Barker (New York: Franklin Watts, 1972).

This book is introduced by calling attention to the Komodo dragon found on the East Island of Komodo. It has black scaly skin that glistens and a forked tongue and weighs three hundred pounds. Thus the book captures readers with dragon stories, including Grimm's "The Dragon's Grandmother."

Holt, David, and Bill Mooney. *Ready-to-Tell Tales: Sure-Fire Stories from America's Favorite Storytellers* (Atlanta, GA: August House, 2005).

Storytellers share one of their favorite stories and advice about how to tell them. Forty-two stories are included.

Justice, Jennifer. *The Ghost and I: Scary Stories for Participation Telling* (Cambridge, MA: Yellow Moon Press, 1992).

Scary ghost stories with a guide to participation and suggestions for proper gestures are provided. Many ideas for adult leaders are found here. From the introduction: "Whether the participation is physically active or in the imagination, being part of a storytelling event brings an audience closer together. Storytelling creates community" (p. 6).

Knudsen, Shannon. *Giants, Trolls and Ogres* (Minneapolis: Lerner Publishing Group, 2010).

Containing unusual explanations and definitions of giants and ogres, this title is surprisingly inclusive for less than fifty pages. Giants of Figi, tall-tale giants, African ogres, and the currently popular Shrek are examples.

Lachman, Lyn Miller. *Multicultural Review* (Ballston Lake, NY).

A quarterly trade journal and book review for educators and librarians examines ethnic and minority information in commentaries and announcements. An interesting article with the title "'I' Is for Inclusion: The Portrayal of Native Americans in Books for Young People" examines titles to avoid and to include and provides sources for good materials.

Leeming, David A., and Marion Sader. *Storytelling Encyclopedia: Historical, Cultural, and Multiethnic Approaches to Oral Traditions around the World* (Phoenix, AZ: Oryx Press, 1997).

Of these five hundred forty-three pages of reference materials, some may be considered outdated, but coverage of many subjects, especially myths and culture, is useful. Also, stories from classic myths from America's tribal nations, Africa, and Asia can be found here.

Lincycomb, Kay. *Storytimes . . . Plus!* (New York: Neal Schuman, 2007).

These plans for storytime are designed for libraries but may be used by others. Thirty-five complete storytimes are outlined, with themes including trains, foods, friends, lizards, rainbow day, and turkey trot. Outlines list story picks, activities, foods, and crafts.

Lopez, Asbel. "Weaving Magic with the Spoken Word," *UNESCO Courier*, May 2001, 54:5, p. 41.

The article describes the art of storytelling in Latin America, including the importance of oral communications, pride in oral heritage, use of narrative tricks, role of tradition in the lives of Haitians, and weaving magic with the spoken word. Described is the International Congress of Oral Storytelling, held since 1995 as part of the Buenos Aires Book Fair. Hundreds of people gather to hear stories and also learn how to tell them—those subtle tricks of toning, voice, and facial expressions. Teachers are included in the festivities. See http://www.questia.com/library/1G1-75143889/weaving-magic-with-the-spoken-word.

Matthew, Kathryn I., and Joy L. Lowe. *Guide to Celebrations and Holidays around the World: The Best Books, Media and Multicultural Learning Activities* (New York: Neal Schuman, 2004).

Books and tales for celebrations and special days occurring in every month of the year are listed for leaders. Ideas for combining activities and crafts with storytelling presentations, lessons, and programs are given.

Miller, Teresa. *Joining In: An Anthology of Audience Participation Stories.* With assistance from Anne Pellowski; Norma Livo, ed.; introduction by Laura Simms (Cambridge, MA: Yellow Moon Press, 1988).

Eighteen stories from various cultures that lend themselves to audience involvement.

Mooney, Bill, and David Holt. *The Storyteller's Guide: Storytellers Share Advice from the Classroom, the Boardroom, Podium, Pulpit and Center Stage* (Atlanta, GA: August House, 1996).

As indicated by the title, advice is offered on varieties of subjects, including beginner's mistakes, stagefright, and frequently asked questions.

Naidoo, Jamie Campbell. *Celebrating Cuentos: Promoting Latino Children's Literature and Literacy in Classrooms and Libraries* (Santa Barbara, CA: Libraries Unlimited, 2010).

Focus here is on informational and cultural needs of Latino students. History, methods, and resources for working with various Spanish-speaking groups are provided. An important essay of interest to storytellers is Lucia M. Gonzales's "Storytelling and Recently Arrived Latino Children," pp. 213–25.

Nanogak (Goose), Agnes. *More Tales from the Igloo* (Toronto: McClelland and Stewart, 1999).

This colorful collection of Inuit legend includes beast tales and hero tales. Stories of the region explain the creation of both physical and spiritual universes.

Norton, Donna E., with Sandra E. Norton. *Through the Eyes of Children: An Introduction to Children's Literature*, 5th ed. (Upper Saddle River, NJ: Prentice Hall, 1995).

A textbook used often to teach children's literature in universities. Included is information on storytelling and folklore.

Pellowski, Anne. *Drawing Stories from Around the World and a Sampling of European Handkerchief Stories* (Westport, CT: Libraries Unlimited, 2005).

A unique presentation of thirty ready-to-tell drawing stories is collected here. Pellowski collected these in travels to Indonesia, Korea, Germany, Romania, Sweden, and Japan. Step-by-step directions are given.

Pellowski, Anne. *The World of Storytelling, Expanded and Revised Edition: A Practical Guide to the Origins, Developments, and Applications of Storytelling* (Bronx, NY: H. W. Wilson, 1990).

A prime source of information and traditions around the world includes a useful multilingual dictionary of terms. The book covers types of storytelling, including bardic, folk, religious, theatrical, library, and campfire; styles of telling, including gestures and voice, musical accompaniment, use of pictures and objects, and openings and closings; and the training of storytellers, including inherited positions, apprenticeships, and informal training. All these elements are compared and contrasted in cultures around the world. Excellent detail, scholarly, and practical.

Perez, Elvia, Margaret Read MacDonald, and Paula Martin. *From the Winds of Manguito: Cuban Folktales in English and Spanish (Desde los Ventos de Manguito: Cuentos Folklorico de Cuba, en Ingles y Espanol)* (Englewood, CO: Libraries Unlimited, 2004).

Twenty-one delightful tales from Hispanic and Afro-Cuban traditions are vibrantly presented in this title. One reviewer describes them by comparing the presentation to Cuba's "intoxicating music" and "delicious foods." In the style of the story series, history of the islands, recipes, and photographs are included.

Philip, Neil. *Mythology of the World: Mighty Gods, Fearsome Goddesses, and Legendary Creatures: Origin and History of the World's Most Captivating Myths* (New York: Kingfisher, 2004).

Lavishly illustrated, with information and stories, the world's mythology is presented in an enticing manner. The notations about various aspects of myths and gods are short, informative, lucid, and appealing. Interesting items about artifacts, myths about the origins of the earth, and myths in relation to festivals and dance capture the imagination. This a perfect title to provoke interest and further discovery. North America, South America, Africa, Europe, Asia, Australia, and Oceania are examined, verifying his claim that "each myth arises from a specific cultural context."

Polette, Nancy. *Fairy Tale Fun* (New York: Neal Schuman, 2011).

Information included should be especially helpful to teachers, with traditional tales from many lands, starting with Aesop's fables and approximately twenty-nine more tales. Included are Hans Christian Andersen's literary tales. For each story, activities and exercises are suggested, such as word search puzzles. Noted are films made from stories and other books and sources for different versions of tales.

Pukui, Mary Kawena, and Laura C. S. Green. *Folktales of Hawaii: He Mau Kaao Hawaii* (Honolulu, HI: Bishop Museum Press, 1995).

Legends of Kawelo and other Hawaiian folktales honor the tradition of storytelling on the islands. Pukui is well known for efforts to preserve

Hawaiian culture and language. Stories are presented in Hawaiian and English in the order of traditional respect: gods, chiefs, and tales of ordinary people.

Saint-Marie, Buffy, et al. "Social Studies: Through Native American Eyes." *Cradleboard Teaching Project* (2002). www.cradleboard.org/curriculum/content.html.

The site provides Native American curriculum to tribal and mainstream schools. Such topics as "Native American Tribal Sovereignty" are presented, complete with lesson plans designed for elementary school through high school.

Sakade, Florence. *Urashima Taro and Other Japanese Children's Stories*. Illus. Yoshio Hayashi (Rutland, VT: Charles E. Tuttle, 1959).

Beginning with the classic lead title, ten tales to tell are included. Most of the stories are retellings of folktales. In a companion book titled *Kintaro's Adventures*, six more narratives are told.

Sanchez, Monica, and Irene Maria F. Blayer, eds. *Storytelling: Interdisciplinary and Intercultural Perspectives* (New York: Peter Lang, 2002).

Themes and motifs of lore are examined.

Sanfield, Steve. *Adventures of High John the Conqueror* (Atlanta, GA: August House, 2006).

Stories about the legendary slave who always outwits "Old Master" are told here. A classic is "The Walking Stick," in which John and master are fishing. Master is bragging about his walking stick. John calls it a stick with "three" ends. Master falls into the trap and promises John a chicken if he can prove the stick has three ends. John points to each end and then throws the stick in the water, where it sinks, the third "end."

Sawyer, Ruth. *The Way of the Storyteller* (New York: Viking, 1942, 1962).

Sawyer's title has been one of the main texts used in university classes teaching storytelling. Her book is a personal statement about her beginnings in a storytelling culture, her training and involvement in the art, and practical advice for storytellers and ends with a selection of stories.

Schank, Roger C. *Tell Me a Story: Narrative and Intelligence* (Evanston, IL: Northwestern University Press, 1990).

Interesting research and thoughts about human intelligence, much of which Schank believes is based in the story, are detailed. He also believes that artificial intelligence will only be perfected when computers are made capable of absorbing the power of a story in all its meanings.

Seale, Doris, and Beverly Slapin. *A Broken Flute: The Native Experience in Books for Children* (Walnut Creek, CA: AltaMira Press, 2005).

Included are enlightening book reviews, stories, poems, and essays valuable for educators, librarians, and storytellers. This is a companion book to *Through Indian Eyes: The Native Experience in Books for Children* (Los Angeles: American Indian Studies Center, University of California, 1998).

Sheppard, Tim. *Traditional Storytelling in Africa.* http://www.timsheppard.co.uk/story/dir/traditions/africa.html.

The FAQ is maintained by Tim Sheppard and can be distributed freely but not for profit. Contained there is a significant amount of information on storytelling and storytelling traditions in various places, including Africa. Names for and status of tellers are listed according to country; roots of some types of tales usually given over to Europe, such as riddle tales; influence of religion; and sources for more reading on specific countries. This website seems to be reputable. Tim Sheppard is a British storyteller and teaches storytelling.

Sherman, Josepha. *Trickster Tales: Forty Folk Stories from Around the World* (Atlanta, GA: August House, 1996).

A collection of multicultural stories about the trickster gives background information on each story. Some unusual folktales are told. One example is "John and His Freedom," about an African American slave who uses trickery to obtain freedom.

Sierra, Judy. *Cinderella.* Illus. Joanne Caroselli (Phoenix, AZ: Oryx, 1992).

Included here are twenty-five variations of the Cinderella motif. Stories are from such disparate places as Egypt, China, Portugal, Iraq, India, and the North American Zuni tribe, and each story is introduced. At the end are a glossary, notes, essays, activities, and resources.

Sierra, Judy, and Robert Kaminski. *Twice upon a Time: Stories to Tell, Retell, Act Out, and Write About* (New York: H. W. Wilson, 1989).

Included are suggestions and outlines for creative dramatics, using the story with music, and other methods accompanying a collection of stories and activities, crafts flannel boards, and more. On page 1 it is stated that "listening to a story told by a storyteller is an intense and exciting experience for a child."

Singer, Isaac. *When Shlemeil Went to Warsaw and Other Stories* (New York: Farrar, Straus, Giroux, 1968).

Eight stories of culture and humor inspired by traditional tales are told by this respected author of Jewish tales. His other books of stories include *Zlateh the Goat, and Other Stories* (New York: Harper and Row, 1966) and *Naftali the Storyteller and His Horse, Sus: And Other Stories* (New York: Farrar, Straus, Giroux, 1976).

Slapin, Beverly, and Doris Seale. *Through Indian Eyes: The Native Experience in Books for Children*, 3rd ed. (Philadelphia: New Society, 1992).

Cultural and historical biases in literary portrayals of tribal nations are vividly presented. Information on stereotypes and what to look for in choosing materials is important for storytellers. Suggested sources for authentic and respectful stories are offered. Jeanette Henry's *A Thousand Years of American Indian Storytelling* (San Francisco: Indian Historian Press, 1981) is highly recommended.

Strom, Karen M. *WWW Virtual Library—American Indians: Index of Native American Resources on the Internet* (2003). www.hanksville.org/NAre-sources.

Strom has compiled another list titled *Native American Themes in Children's and YA Books.* Find this at http://cynthialeitichsmith.com/lit_resources/diversity/native_am/NativeThemes_intro.html.

Sutherland, Zena. *Children and Books.* Illus. Trina Schart Hyman (New York: Addison Wesley Longman. 1997).

For the study of children's literature, history, and use, this title includes an interesting chapter on the origin of folklore, stating that folktales are a "mirror of a people." Sutherland postulates that many tales are "symbols of emotional fantasy, dreams or nightmares and contain remnants of rituals, spells and incantations" (p. 167).

Thompson, Stith. *Motif Index of Folk Literature: A Classification of Narrative Elements in Folktales, Ballads, Myths, Fables, Medieval Romances, Exempla, Fabliaux, Jest Books and Local Legends* (Bloomington: Indiana University Press, 1958).

Stith Thompson has done the most extensive work in classifying tales.

Torrence, Jackie. *The Importance of Pot Liquor,* American Storytelling Series (Atlanta, GA: August House, 1994).

The celebrated storyteller leaves a legacy of lore, some of which are family stories from her childhood. This is the source of the "pot liquor" story. Her grandmother always had a cup from which she drank the broth from cooking greens and other items. North Carolinians and other southerners will be familiar with the folk traditions she shares.

Trelease, Jim. *Hey! Listen to This; Stories to Read Aloud* (New York: Viking, 1992).

By the author of *The New Read-Aloud Handbook* (New York: Penguin Books, 1989), some titles in this anthology are also perfect for telling. Forty-eight stories, including "Uncle Remus Tales" retold by Julius Lester, are included with a variety of fairy tales, folktales, and modern stories.

Vigil, Angel. *The Corn Woman: Stories and Legends of the Hispanic Southwest (La Mujer del Maiz: Cuentos y Leyendas del Sudoeste Hispano)* (Englewood, CO: Libraries Unlimited, 1994).

Forty-five stories from the region, including obscure and well-known tales. These are cultural stories, including animal tales and tales of wisdom. Fifteen are written in Spanish.

Walsh, John. *The Art of Storytelling: Easy Steps to Presenting an Unforgettable Story* (Chicago: Moody, 2003).

The twenty-first century has brought the attention of business and other professions to uses of storytelling. Numerous Internet sites are designed to instruct businessmen in story presentation. This title focuses on the ministry. Most of the tools discussed are familiar, but the accent is on training Christian leaders and others.

Waters, Fiona. *Aesop's Fables.* Illus. Fulvio Testa (London: Andersen Press, 2010).

The fables are retold here with bright colorful illustrations large enough for classroom sharing. The morals are also sometimes reworded. "The Lion and the Mouse" ends with "Sometimes even the strongest person needs a weaker person's help" (p. 16), and the ending of "The Fox and the Grapes" is "Don't belittle things that are beyond your reach out of frustration" (p. 78).

Zipes, Jack, trans. *The Complete Fairy Tales of the Brothers Grimm*, 3rd expanded edition. Illus. John Gruelle (New York: Bantam Books, 2003).

Translated and with an introduction by Zipes, the book begins with a history of the Grimm brothers. Claims are made that this is the most inclusive collection of tales by the Grimms. Included are new tales translated from the annotations and notes of the brothers. One new story is about a simpleton trying to marry the daughter of a very distinguished family. He misinterprets the suggestions given to him by his mother and destroys his chances. She tells him, "Cast your eyes upon her politely and steadily." When the girl arrives, the simpleton throws a handful of animal eyes at her. The folklorist Jack Zipes is a professor of German at the University of Wisconsin.

Index

About the Author

Binnie Tate Wilkin has been a storyteller throughout her multifaceted career. Her presentations of African and American stories are still in demand. Yearly, she fulfills a standing invitation to entertain the public at the Los Angeles County Library's Juneteenth celebration held at the A. C. Bilbrew Branch Library. After completing her master's degree in library science at the State University of New York at Albany, Ms. Wilkin was a school librarian and a children's librarian. As children's specialist for the Los Angeles City Library, she received national attention for her creative participation in that library's federally funded outreach project. Subsequently, after writing several articles in library literature, Binnie Tate Wilkin was recruited to lecture at library schools throughout the country, including the University of Wisconsin, Milwaukee; California State University, Fullerton; the University of California, at Los Angeles and at Berkeley; and the University of Hawaii, Honolulu. Courses taught include "Children's Literature," "Children's Services," "Young Adult Services," "Minority Services," "Public Libraries," and "Storytelling." In October 1996, Ms. Wilkin received a Professional Achievement Award from the Black Caucus of the American Library Association. At the American Library Association's First National Joint Conference of Librarians of Color in 2006, she received an Outstanding Achievement Award from the cooperating minority caucuses. Ms. Wilkin worked on numerous committees and has done consultant work for the American Library Association.

Binnie Tate Wilkin has authored several well-received professional articles. Her essay "In Retrospect and Forward: Issues Facing Black Librarians" appears in the 2012 Scarecrow Press book *The 21st Century Black Librarian in America: Issues and Challenges*. The second edition of Wilkin's book *Survival Themes in Fiction for Children and Young People* was published by Scarecrow Press in 1994. Her most recent publications are *African American Librarians in the Far West: Pioneers and Trailblazers*, released by Scarecrow Press in July 2006, and *African and American Images in Newbery Award–Winning Titles: Progress in Portrayals*, published in August 2009. Ms. Wilkin has told stories nationally and internationally.